As a leader, you must be a master of intent;
those on your team are masters of interpretation.

Match your intent to what you want
your team to interpret.

YOU
HAVE
WHAT
IT TAKES

USING THE SKILLS YOU HAVE TO EXCEL IN LEADERSHIP

KELLY GIBBONS

You Have What It Takes
Using the Skills You Have to Excel in Leadership
Kelly Gibbons © 2024

Print ISBN: 978-1-61206-309-6
eBook ISBN: 978-1-61206-310-2

To purchase this book at quantity discounts, contact Aloha Publishing at alohapublishing@gmail.com

Published by

Printed in the United States of America

This book is dedicated to my parents, Chuck and Trudy Gibbons.
They provided perspective from both sides of every coin,
allowing me to take ownership of my life's journey.

CONTENTS

FOREWORD

You Have What It Takes isn't just another leadership book. Nope, it's a breath of fresh air in a crowded room that emphasizes all the ways your leadership journey is unique to you. This book, written by my brilliant friend, Kelly Gibbons, grabs you by the shoulders, looks you in the eye, and says, "Hey, today begins your leadership journey. It's yours and nobody else's. Embrace it."

As you crack open the first chapter, Kelly's voice echoes through the pages, urging readers to leverage authenticity. "Just do you," she is whispering. She's not about copying someone else's style; she's all for finding your own groove. This message lays the foundation for a leadership approach grounded in self-awareness and the courage to be true to yourself.

Throughout the book, you'll find that Kelly is like that wise friend who knows when to push you into the deep end—gently, of course. She talks about looking in the mirror, *really looking*, and finding what makes you shine and where you might need a bit of polishing. Use her words as a roadmap for recognizing strengths and embracing vulnerabilities. Stepping beyond comfort zones and learning from failure will lead to resilience and growth—it's in these moments of challenge and reflection that true leaders are built.

Your journey through the book is like taking a master class in being human. You will find nuanced insights on emotional intelligence, discover the confidence to face adversity head-on, and understand the importance of trusting your instincts. And the ultimate message rings loud and clear: leadership isn't about the accolades; it's about the impact we make. It's about the high fives doled out for the wins and the pats on the back for times we tried and didn't quite get there.

To leaders everywhere, may this book inspire you to pursue your unique leadership journey with courage and confidence. Kelly, through her continued guidance, will be right there, cheering you on and reminding you that, yep, you've got what it takes!

With belief in your potential and a big smile,

Allison Dunn
Executive Business Coach, Deliberate Directions

INTRODUCTION

If you've ever struggled to find the confidence you need to lead effectively, you're not alone. I've become very confident in my abilities as a coach and as a leader, and while that confidence may have been innate, it wasn't automatic; it took a great deal of effort, fueled by determination and failure, to get there.

My first year of coaching sports at a collegiate level felt, at least to me, like a failure. My team didn't have as much success as I'd hoped, and I began to question my ability because of my youth and inexperience in the college coaching environment.

I made many mistakes during that time, but rarely did I make them twice. Unfortunately, some of those mistakes were placing trust in untrustworthy people or situations. My ability to trust shrank, and I became very wary of others. I spent a great deal of time searching for outside approval for my decisions because I didn't trust myself, which was exhausting.

It eventually became clear that I was doing my team and myself a disservice by concerning myself with the opinions of people who had no stake in the game. I had to learn to trust myself more, to coach with integrity and intention.

When you're able to trust yourself, it becomes much more apparent who is trustworthy and it also becomes easier for others to trust you.

The process of learning how to lead never stops. While some of us have a natural inclination toward coaching and leadership, it's still something that must be studied in order to develop. I've found that the most memorable lessons and experiences were those where I discovered the answers to my questions for myself. Every time I did so, I was able to achieve more and help others achieve more than anyone had thought possible.

Everyone has innate qualities that contribute to the way they lead. These are formed from your natural personality traits, skills you've practiced throughout your life, experiences you've had, and challenges you've overcome.

If you're like me and many other leaders, you've likely come across a situation in your leadership you felt unequipped to handle because you felt you lacked the skills, knowledge, or simply the confidence. These situations are some of the most difficult to face as a leader, but when you understand your innate qualities and your leadership style well, you'll often find you already have what it takes.

My goal is to help you develop self-awareness to understand the strengths you already have, the obstacles you've faced that have given you tools to use in leadership, and where you can find resources and assistance when you need it.

Understand that, right now, you likely have what it takes to accomplish what you want.

Experiential leadership is a resourceful form of leadership that allows you to discover the answers to questions for yourself and lead from a place of awareness of your own strengths and challenges. This method of leadership helps you build confidence in yourself and your skills so you're able to approach new experiences with the knowledge that you're capable of navigating it.

When you understand yourself well, you can lead from a heartfelt position with self-awareness and self-empowerment. Understanding your own qualities leads to better confidence as a leader and helps you create a positive environment where people can grow and perform their best. When you're aware of your strengths, you can act without doubt and know where you need to seek assistance or additional resources to supplement areas where you question your abilities.

By the end of this book, you should be able to approach almost any challenge by asking yourself, "How can I draw from what I have already?"

Right now, you likely have what it takes to accomplish what you want.

Experiential leadership starts with curiosity. In order to build self-awareness, you must be curious enough to ask questions. When I went to college, I was always asking questions of my instructors and coaches, driven by the same curiosity that prompted me to keep opening books as a child. And my favorite question was "Why?"

Frequently, I'd receive a reply you might have heard from your own parent: "Because I told you to." Those words discourage curiosity and learning—they are about establishing a power dynamic rather than teaching. As a result, I vowed I would never use that line as a coach or parent—ever! In contrast, when I did get satisfactory answers to my questions, I would absorb the information, ask clarifying questions, make a better connection with the coach or teacher, and finally execute whatever was being asked of me.

A questioning, curious attitude gets more accomplished than blind compliance. It's important for leaders to stay curious. There's always something you can learn from those you lead, from mentors, and perhaps most importantly, from yourself.

As you approach the concepts in this book, keep that question in the back of your mind in capital letters: WHY? Ask this question to try on your personal answer for each concept you engage with throughout the book. Stay curious.

In my approach to coaching, I'm passionate about learning and teaching, but most importantly about empowerment. I excelled early in my sports career because I became a student of each game. I learned as much as I could from my father, who played basketball and softball, and he would talk strategy with me. By the time I was 16, I was not only playing sports but coaching as well in a youth group of summer softball players. That summer lit a fire for coaching and my future leadership.

As an executive leadership coach, I've worked with many leaders who don't realize they already have what it takes to lead effectively and with confidence. I've held a wide variety of leadership positions, from sports coaching to C-suite roles across different industries, including nonprofit organizations, university programs, and healthcare administration. All along the way, I learned and adapted by asking questions and discovering resources that were already available to me.

However, I couldn't call my coaching my own until I stopped simply assimilating information and began forging a path unique to me. I had to take all the answers to my questions and use them to form a personalized leadership style that leveraged my unique strengths and experiences to lead effectively. That path was slowly created through a series of *aha* moments, which I will share with you throughout this book.

My goal is to help you think through your own leadership style using your personal experience and strengths. In order to do so, you will need to identify what guides you—the answers to your personal "why" questions.

Experiential leadership will help you build stronger and more resilient teams, able to truly work together and solve problems—and you'll have the resources and the confidence you need to face any challenge, even one that's outside your expertise.

CHAPTER 1

Discover Your Unique Leadership Style

"People don't really learn when you tell them something. They don't really learn when they do something. People start learning, start creating neural pathways, only when they have a chance to recall and reflect on what just happened."

–Michael Bungay Stanier, *The Coaching Habit*

Leadership may be more natural to you than you think. Many of us don't realize we have the natural skills we need to succeed, gained through a wealth of life experiences. We just have to stop and ask ourselves the right questions.

Every leader needs a leadership strategy, and it can make the difference between leading confidently or feeling as though you're not a good leader. Many leaders don't realize they already have what it takes because they don't have a strong leadership strategy based in their own skills and experience.

Aha Moment

Experiential leadership is about developing your own leadership style based on emotional intelligence and skills you already have, creating a leadership style that is personalized and adaptable to any situation.

While there are many leadership and coaching systems others have created that you can follow, even the most highly effective methods have limits and won't be applicable to every situation. Many leaders make the mistake of ascribing their success to someone else's methods rather than their own personal and accountable leadership journey. And if you haven't developed confidence in your own leadership style, it may seem easiest or most effective to adopt someone else's proven methods. However, this approach makes failure less of a learning opportunity and instead encourages placing blame on others. It also makes it more difficult to adapt to change, as these leaders don't own the leadership process they're using. When something goes wrong, rather than using their own skills and experience to solve the problem, they look for another template to fix it.

New leaders tend to grasp at the success of others rather than owning their personal strengths and developing their own leadership style. However, this sets them up for failure because they're relying on others for solutions and practicing leadership outside their personal strengths, experience, and expertise, and they lack the tools to navigate challenges in this unknown territory.

Experiential leadership creates a more adaptable model of leadership that is built on self-awareness, allowing the leader to make confident decisions by understanding their own motivations and skills and knowing when and where to seek appropriate help.

Part of the beauty of experiential leadership is that when leaders understand themselves better and are able to build a personal leadership model that works for them, they're also better able to guide their team members to reflect on their own experiences. Learning to develop their leadership skills allows them to help individuals and whole teams succeed.

THE ROLE OF A LEADER

I learned to lead through the practice of coaching, and I believe coaching is heavily intertwined with great leadership. The most important role of a coach is to be a mentor, which requires you to let go of your ego. A successful leader has a high level of emotional intelligence and a sense of internal integrity, leading authentically rather than selling out to someone else's views or values. It requires you to be true to yourself and what you believe is important. Successful leaders are able to see the big picture in parts and pieces, to visualize how all the smaller aspects of a team—and of the individuals on the team—function to form the bigger picture. If you're leading people, you have to be able to see who is able to fill a part and where people fit, as well as what to adjust when things aren't working the way they need to.

Find tools and methods that don't just support what you're already doing but enrich what you're doing, tools that you can adapt and make your own. I choose to incorporate things I learn that mean something to me rather than adopting a method wholesale. What does what you're learning mean to you, and can you speak to it if it doesn't speak to you or if you haven't implemented it? If you tell your team to do something they've never tried when you've also never tried it, that's very inauthentic, and it will be difficult to get the buy-in you need from your team.

DISCOVER THE TOOLS YOU ALREADY HAVE

So what does experiential leadership look like, and what steps can you take to get there?

Start by asking questions. Remember my favorite question—"why?" Understanding your "why" in everything you do—and everything you ask your team to do—will give you clarity in your choices and how you approach each situation.

Keep leadership personal. You do you. No method you adopt from someone else's success will be as effective as the methods you know work for you. You already have the tools you need to succeed. Of course, we don't always know what our own skills and strengths are, and discovering them requires self-reflection. Over the next few chapters, I'll take you through the process of looking back on your experiences to find those tools and evaluate the skills you've learned from past experiences, your passions, and your vision that will guide you as you lead.

Each of us has a toolbox we carry with us all the time and add to as we gain new knowledge and experiences. For example, in my toolbox I carry all my parenting skills, which are assimilated from all the parents and people I've been around, both negative and positive, and all that I've learned and read. And I pull from those tools with my kids and my grandkids. I've gotten extremely comfortable with those tools because they're tried and true.

Leadership certainly isn't new, and there's plenty of wisdom to be gained by looking back on what has helped people in the past succeed. It's wise to draw from that. We don't have to reinvent leadership for every person. With all of the templates and principles and strategies that are available, you have so much to choose from. But you can't make all of them work, and some of them won't work for you at all. But when you understand the tools you already have, you can determine how to use the wisdom of past leaders to hone those tools and make them even better.

Aha Moment

Recognizing your own tools and experience gives you confidence to use them in new areas rather than saying, "I can't do that because I've never done it before."

You already have what it takes, too, and recognizing that starts by identifying your strengths.

LOOKING BACK

Many of us don't recognize the valuable skills and experience we already have—that's why we have to look back and reflect carefully to find it.

Each person's leadership style is unique because we all approach problems with different perspectives and approaches based on our experiences and what has worked for us in the past. From a very young age, you begin to form methods of thinking and problem-solving that help you navigate your world. Those experiences continue to inform the way you think throughout your life, even while you continue to adapt and learn from each new situation.

When it comes to solving a specific problem that's different from what you've experienced before in specific ways, it's easy to become intimidated or lack confidence in your own abilities. You may be inclined to focus on all the elements that are *different* from your experiences rather than the ones that are the same. After all, what works for one situation may not be appropriate in another, and it takes skill and emotional intelligence to understand when principles that work in one area can be applied to another.

However, learning to recognize the skills you have from past experiences that may not be related to leadership can help you identify skills you can easily adapt to suit your leadership needs. Our experiences lend us emotional intelligence, interpersonal skills, creative problem-solving abilities, and many other helpful traits. And luckily, as humans, we're very good at adapting the principles that worked for us in one situation to another.

Look for learning experiences you've had at all ages and stages, whether that was the lesson of stranger-danger and steering clear of aggressive animals as a child, to learning to bake a pie or ice-skate for the first time. All of these valuable lessons may not seem related to leadership, but they contain principles that can be applied in different ways. If you had to fall over 20 times before you could make it around the ice skating rink and finally have fun on the ice, then you learned the value of perseverance. In baking your first pie, you may have learned the importance of reading instructions before starting a project. Those skills are things you still use on a regular basis.

One of the most valuable types of experience to draw from is family relationships. They teach us a great deal about interpersonal skills, emotional intelligence, and human nature. They teach us various methods of interacting with others—sharing, taking turns, and letting someone else shine. Things we learned in kindergarten are reinforced through family relationships throughout our lives. Those relationships play a major role in shaping us as individuals and as leaders.

If you're a parent, chances are you've gained a great deal of leadership skills through parenting. Coaching is like parenting in many ways—helping your team members create habits, providing them with consistent information, and helping them form healthy and respectful relationships with their team (or the family). Even if you're not a parent, your own parents provided examples of leadership—positive or negative—that influenced the way you think.

By looking back and identifying methods that have worked for you in other areas of life, you'll find yourself better equipped to approach new challenges even if you don't have specific knowledge or experience of the situation by adapting and applying those skills and principles.

Learning from your experiences doesn't stop with reflection. We're all having new experiences every day. Pay attention to what you are learning because you never know when you will need it. Everything is an opportunity to learn from in your life.

Adopt a Positive Lens

When looking back at your experiences, it's important to view them from a positive lens. You can gain a great deal from both positive and negative experiences, and both are necessary. It's in reflection that you learn from your experiences, and you must be willing to examine a negative experience with the intent to discover the positive things that arose from it.

As I started my coaching career, I quickly realized I had much to learn. In my years as a player, I had four volleyball coaches. It was the coach at a high school volleyball camp who made the biggest impact on me. Her example of coaching and playing inspired me, and I began devoting myself to perfecting my own skills in volleyball, while I'd previously been focused on basketball. My playing career took an entirely new trajectory as I became intensely focused on volleyball. She opened my eyes to what I could do with the game and what the game could do for me. As a result of my newfound focus and intensity on my abilities, a year later I was offered a full-ride scholarship to the University of Idaho for volleyball and to Washington State University for basketball. My choice to go to Idaho was a good fit.

However, my coach during my senior year in college was a train wreck. Through that experience, I discovered that just as much growth can come from adversity and bad leadership. You have to adjust your mindset to allow it to flow that way. I learned ways I *didn't* want to interact, ways I *didn't* want to lead. I saw many of those traits in other supervisors I have had over the years. I value what they teach me and then I adapt and adopt those tenants, which produce results. I smiled as I walked to the podium while being inducted into the Hall of Fame at the

26

University of Idaho, decades later, proving you can still succeed in spite of poor leadership—even though it's not ideal.

It was not a clean process, however, and I also adopted some poor ideologies from the wreckage. Over the years, my players and coachees have helped me figure out how to be authentic with my unique style and nurture attributes in myself and others that create empowerment.

It is important to have opportunities to work with leaders who are not as effective. It is a chance to understand what you don't want to be and to truly capture your authentic self by discovering what you don't want to adopt. But in order to gain from those experiences, you must reflect on them with a positive lens.

THE ANSWER IS A QUESTION

Discovering that you have what it takes requires curiosity. It is only by asking yourself the right questions that you can discover the skills, experience, and motivations needed to develop your own experiential leadership style and gain the confidence necessary to lead effectively.

Start by answering these questions:

- What are you doing?
- Why are you doing it?
- What motivates you?
- Why get involved?
- Why take that extra step?
- What's next?
- How will you go forward from here?

- What's your role? Are you in the way of your team's success, or are you an important cog in their functions?

- What questions do you need to ask yourself?

- What questions do you need to ask others?

Questions like these lead to the next level of learning and the next level of leading by increasing your self-awareness.

When you know you have what it takes, you may not know the questions yet, but you know you'll be able to find the answers. You're comfortable with the answers you've been able to give up until now, so you're ready for the next question, whatever it happens to be.

You'll always encounter new questions that you haven't thought about, questions that will challenge you. But if you have the confidence of knowing you have what it takes, you'll be prepared to face those questions and explore their answers, even if it takes you in an unexpected direction.

If you're grounded in knowing you have what it takes and understanding your reasons behind everything you do, what supports you, and what drives you, you'll be ready for any kind of question or challenge that comes your way.

The Power of the Question

The best leaders don't have the right answers—they have the right questions. The questions you ask as a leader, and the manner in which you ask them, has an incredible power to shape thoughts, conversations, and feelings. The answers you get can reveal important information to guide you in decision-making.

But asking good questions requires confidence. People with a low level of confidence may try to boost their self-image by speaking quickly in response to a question or pretending to have all the answers even if those answers aren't very well thought-out. But it takes real confidence to ask questions rather than answering them and then to listen—really listen.

Aha Moment

A good leader doesn't have to have the answers.
They can look to their team to bring them the answers.

Rather than giving answers to those they lead, they ask questions to help their team members find their own answers. And that's how leaders grow team members into leaders in their own right, by empowering individuals to answer them and trusting that they have the answer or the tools and the skills to dig it up.

The better you become at asking questions, the more confidence you'll build because you don't have to have all the answers and you can be okay with that. Instead, you've got the ability to ask great questions and listen for the right answers.

TAKEAWAYS

- Experiential leadership is developing a personalized and adaptable leadership style based on experience, emotional intelligence, and interpersonal skills you already have and will continue to develop.

- You already have what it takes to lead effectively. Start by identifying your strengths in order to build confidence in your own abilities.

- You can gain a great deal from both positive and negative experiences, but you must be willing to examine a negative experience with the intent to discover the positive things that arose from it.

- Focus on asking good questions rather than having all the answers. A confident leader understands how to ask the right questions to listen for and find the answers they need.

CHAPTER 2

Increase Self-Awareness

"Authenticity is about being true to who you are, even when everyone around you wants you to be someone else."

–Michael Jordan

Becoming a better leader requires self-awareness to understand your own skills, motivations, and challenges. Self-awareness allows you to discover why you have the skills you do, where you lead well, where you underestimate yourself, and how others respond to your attitudes and behaviors.

Leaders with high levels of self-awareness have more tools to lead effectively and tend to be more confident in their abilities. It's natural to think you know yourself well, but self-awareness doesn't happen without significant work, and people are very good at creating self-images in their minds that don't reflect reality. We all do it to some extent, and learning to take apart those self-images to discover what's true about yourself leads to a more accurate understanding of the self and enables growth. It's not until you stop and examine your thoughts, habits, and past experiences that you can truly become self-aware.

In his book *Atomic Habits*, James Clear wrote, "What comes naturally to me? For just a moment, ignore what you have been taught. Ignore what society has told you. Ignore what others expect of you. Look inside yourself and ask, 'What feels natural to me? When have I felt alive? When have I felt like the real me?' No internal judgments or people-pleasing. No second-guessing or self-criticism. Just feelings of engagement and enjoyment. Whenever you feel authentic and genuine, you are headed in the right direction."

Even once you've become confident in who you are, what motivates you, and what you're good at, to be a strong leader you must continue to interrogate your thoughts, feelings, and experiences. The journey toward self-awareness does not have a destination or end point because as humans, we are constantly changing, learning, and growing, and we must remain aware of the ways in which we've changed.

SELF-AWARENESS AS A LEADERSHIP TRAIT

When I was a senior in college, I had a coach who lacked self-awareness and had no idea what effects she was having on the team. She was inexperienced and thought she knew much more than she did. She'd moved from player to assistant coach to head coach in the same institution, which to me is a recipe for disaster because there's nothing motivating you to do anything different than what you've done in the past. My team had gotten into the swing of things before she took over, and she was gifted a well-oiled team. She took credit for their success, and the next year when the senior leadership left, it was a very challenging year for the team.

Without self-awareness, it's impossible to grow. It lends vital perspective in determining where growth is needed and helps you receive both positive and negative feedback without judgment.

Self-awareness requires the willingness to examine yourself with an outside perspective and put aside self-interest, judgment, and limiting beliefs. When you have a realistic view of yourself, you're better able to recognize positive and negative traits, skills, habits, and beliefs.

Learning to be self-aware also requires critical thinking, which can help you understand others and grow your emotional intelligence. It's impossible to effectively lead people you don't understand, and by learning to think critically about yourself, you can help others do the same.

Knowing yourself allows you to create your own leadership strategy that's based in your strengths. You'll discover the tools you already have that can be applied to your leadership approach. And when you find a method that leads to success, that's something you can duplicate and incorporate into your overall strategy.

Self-awareness gives you a foundation for your leadership strategy. That strategy has to be your own, based on your own experiences and skills. If you stray too far outside your own experience, you'll eventually run into a wall.

In my nonprofit work, I once worked under a very self-aware boss who knew her strengths and where she needed support, and she hired me to fill a new position she'd created. Soon after hiring me, she discovered more of my strengths and adjusted my responsibilities to fit my skills. She empowered and encouraged me to take on some of her tasks. She was never worried about who would receive credit for the job, as long as it was done with high standards of accountability. Her self-awareness helped me develop my emotional intelligence.

Aha Moment

Leaders who are aware of their strengths and challenges are better able to recognize the strengths and challenges of others and adapt as needed.

THE STORIES WE TELL OURSELVES

We all tell ourselves stories about who we are, what we are and aren't good at, and what we should and shouldn't do because of it.

Have you ever heard someone object to being assigned a task by saying, "I'm not creative"? Or maybe that's even you! In doing so, they shut down any opportunity to learn. The truth is everyone is creative. Everyone has something they can create. But people pigeonhole the definition of creative into specific skills like drawing or building things rather than just the creativity of discovering an opportunity or solving a problem. And by telling themselves they're not creative, they construct a self-narrative that makes them feel as if they *can't* be creative. That negative self-narrative keeps them from trying, from working to become better at creativity, or even from succeeding at creative endeavors where they may actually be skilled. Instead, they've internalized "not creative" as part of their identity.

If you view yourself as a person who is not creative, you won't be able to see all the ways in which you already are creative and the creative potential you have to achieve things you may not have thought possible.

Unfortunately, many people do the exact same thing with leadership—they say, "I'm not a good leader." Maybe they've had some negative feedback or haven't been challenged as a leader in a positive way. Maybe they've adopted someone else's leadership style that hasn't worked for them.

Let's say you're reading a book on leadership that describes methods to lead successfully. If you use those methods with your team, following the book to the letter, it can come across as inauthentic. Your team may wonder if you really believe the methods you're following or if you're simply regurgitating information. But just because the leadership strategies you've been given haven't worked well for you doesn't mean you're a bad leader. Instead, think critically about the leadership principles and tools you adopt. Some may not apply well to you or your situation. Some may need to be adapted and others disregarded.

I've seen this happen repeatedly in sports. I've brought in top recruits who'd played limited roles in high school and were very good at their specialized positions—middle hitters in volleyball, for example. They'd come into preseason training camp and couldn't pass a ball to save their soul because all they did in high school was hit and block on the front row.

If all they have done is hit, they may think or may have been told they're not a passer. I've had plenty of athletes in my college program tell me what they do and what they don't do, and I always ask, "Well, have you ever tried?"

The response often is, "Yeah, but I really suck at it."

The problem is that these athletes haven't allowed themselves to be challenged, so they default to the excuse of "I'm not good at it." It makes their decisions easier, because they've been given or taken on that label, not just as what they *do* but who they *are*—"I'm not a passer."

However, if that athlete refuses to get better at passing, that means someone else has to take responsibility for passing. And often, that's the reason they've taken on that label—they don't want the responsibility. Another motivator is that these athletes don't want to look foolish playing outside of their realm of expertise. The same goes for leaders. I've seen leaders who are great at running exercises at leadership conferences but don't want to be asked to speak in front of an audience.

Women in particular tend to fall into this mental trap of believing they're not capable of something. Of course men do it too, but I see it more commonly in women, saying things like, "I can't do that!" even when they may be able to complete the task in question quite well. They possess a label, self-imposed or imposed by someone else, that limits them.

As leaders, we must be able to identify our limiting beliefs and overcome them. If someone is having difficulty seeing themselves in a leadership position, my first coaching strategy is to understand where that limiting belief is coming from: "What brings you to that conclusion?"

PRACTICING SELF-AWARENESS

Start by identifying a limiting belief or self-narrative. Are you not cut out to be a leader? Are you bad at creative or artistic pursuits?

Do you believe you're not athletic, or that you're terrible at public speaking?

Once you've identified your limiting belief, ask yourself this: What brings you to that conclusion? Did someone say that to you at some point? Did you have a bad experience where you panicked and froze, or failed despite trying? Chances are you had an experience of some sort that led to that limiting belief.

Next, reflect on a time when you had success at something relating to that belief. Look at things you've produced or achieved. What made those situations different? What can you learn from it?

Even if that limiting belief is true in the present (and it may not be), that doesn't mean it will remain true forever. Humans are remarkable at developing new skills, but our limiting beliefs often keep us from challenging ourselves. Where can you find tools to help you get better at that skill? Start doing the research. Look for different perspectives than your own. You don't necessarily have to adopt those tools or perspectives—you already know how I feel about leadership templates. But chances are you'll find some nugget that gives you a place to start and adapt new methods for yourself.

It's never too late to start learning new skills to become a better leader. "I'm too old to change now" is just one more limiting belief that excuses you from taking responsibility to learn and to become a better leader and team player.

Self-awareness of your limiting beliefs opens a whole new avenue of opportunity. In places where you previously may have shut down opportunities for growth because you've had bad experiences in the past, you can work to understand where those beliefs come from and how they're limiting you. Knowing the source of the beliefs allows you to begin deconstructing those beliefs, taking them apart and discovering what skills you have and how you can apply them in new ways. Maybe you're really great at A and B, but you've always told yourself you suck at C. Well, some of the skills you use for A and B actually apply to C.

For me, this is a lot like cooking. I have a couple of meals I can make in my sleep. But sometimes I challenge myself to cook something entirely new. It's probably going to look bad, but at least it will taste good. However to get that good-tasting meal, I have to be willing to try rather than telling myself I'm a terrible cook or that I'm only good at cooking certain things. And maybe the reason I'm not a fantastic cook is because I've never really challenged myself or I've never had the opportunity to use great ingredients or cook in a high-tech kitchen, so I tend to just cook easy and convenient foods.

The same goes for leadership. You have to be willing to try new things and apply skills you have from other areas of life. And just because you've failed at something before or have had a negative experience doesn't mean you can't improve.

Increasing your self-awareness as a whole will help you challenge limiting self-beliefs by rooting your self-identity in facts rather than assumptions. The better you know yourself, not only from your own internal perspective but also from outside perspectives, the better you'll be able to combat limiting beliefs.

GROWING YOUR SELF-AWARENESS

As you gain self-awareness, you'll discover that some leadership skills may be more natural to you than you realize. Growing self-awareness begins by looking back—recalling experiences and opportunities in your past where you were impactful, even if it was unplanned. Whatever challenge you may face, chances are you've had an experience that mirrors at least some aspects of it in the past.

Think both inside and outside the leadership sphere. Experiences from other parts of life can be just as valuable. Maybe you successfully dissolved a tense family situation over Thanksgiving dinner, or you were able to creatively solve a problem at work when you weren't in a leadership position.

You gain insight into your strengths by illustrating to yourself how you've succeeded in the past. When you're faced with a challenge you don't feel confident handling, that's a cue it's time to look back to discover the tools you have to help you approach the situation.

Looking back helps you find where you lead well and where you fall short. Maybe you have some excellent parenting skills that can be applied to leadership, but struggle with certain aspects of communication or problem-solving. Through this process, you can uncover the skills you have and *why* you have the skills you do, which improves your confidence in your abilities. It also helps you learn where you underestimate yourself.

Any time you reach a conclusion that you're not good at something, challenge that assumption. Ask yourself what brings you to the conclusion that you're not good at that skill. Then begin to examine what you've done in the past. How have you managed to get past related challenges? What tools do you already have that apply to that skill set?

Finally, ask yourself why you're holding onto that belief. Is it true, or is it a limiting self-perception? Often you *do* have the tools necessary; they're just different than the tools other leaders use. The leadership strategy that works for you will be based in your own strengths. And when you identify a real challenge you have, that will also help you become a stronger leader by knowing when to turn to resources outside yourself, as well as pointing out an opportunity for growth.

It's a good habit to revisit your past experiences on a regular basis. Doing so helps you create a sort of library of experiences or memories in your mind that you can draw from when needed. For example, when I was hired at my second college coaching job for softball, I not only revisited my files of preseason game prep, but I recalled situations I anticipated encountering again, such as recruiting. I was able to reflect on which behaviors were more or less effective or meaningful and was able to adapt my approach to create more successful outcomes.

Reflecting on your past experiences gives you valuable insight into the present and helps you strategize for the future. And the more frequently you practice this, building your library of experiences, the easier it will come to you and the more confident you'll feel in your decisions.

KNOW YOUR OWN GOALS

It's easy to look at what someone else has achieved and think, "I want that; that's my goal." But when you do that, you end up working toward someone else's goals rather than your own, and in the process, you set yourself up for disappointment and most likely failure. The truth is you don't have to have the same goals or abilities as others to be a successful leader.

As a young leader, I was very impressionable and tended to adopt strategies that had worked for others in hopes of achieving the same successes. But I didn't have a filter for how those methods would work for me. I didn't stop to think, "If that's my destination, maybe there's another way to get there." Instead, it was as though I was chasing a train, following in the tracks of someone moving on a trajectory I couldn't catch up to, even though I wanted to go to the same destination.

When I learned to narrow my own goals to focus on the things that mattered most to me, I realized I could make a much bigger impact in my life and in the world around me. If all I did my whole career was help leaders develop their leadership strategy, I'd be making a huge impact.

Self-awareness is critical because without it, you might be shooting at the wrong goal entirely, trying to grab onto someone else's coattails. You must cross your own bridges.

NEW GOALS ARE A NEGOTIATION

True leaders are constantly learning, and their goals are constantly evolving. If you have a single goal with a set end point, what happens when you reach it? You become lost or complacent without something on the horizon to continue moving toward. Forward movement is essential to leadership.

However, because many leaders are highly goal-oriented, as your goals evolve, it can be easy to begin piling them on. Chances are you want to accomplish many things in your life, and the reality is that you can only dedicate yourself to a few of them.

Aha Moment

Creating goals is a negotiation. New goals are not add-ons—they are exchanges.

No matter where you are in your life, new goals always require negotiation with the self—for your energy, time, and resources. Regardless of how busy you are, taking on something new will always require you to sacrifice something that's a current part of your routine, to change your focus. And if you take on new goals without first examining and planning for what you'll need to sacrifice in order to achieve them, it may result in letting something with a higher priority slip by the wayside.

Knowing yourself and which goals are your highest priorities—the ones that are truly yours and not others' goals that you've adopted—will guide you in negotiating to discover whether and where new goals fit into your life.

KNOW WHAT GUIDES YOU

One of the most critical parts of self-awareness is understanding what guides you—your beliefs, motivations, values, and personal limits that influence the decisions you make every day.

Examine the things that guide you to better understand the leadership strategies that will work for you. So how do you discover the guiding forces in your life?

Start by asking yourself these questions to discover what you value:

- Who do you respect?

- Who impresses you and why? What are they doing that makes you pause and notice?

- What can you learn from them?

Another factor in what guides you are your personal limits. Knowing your limits can help you strategize and plan your approach to various challenges to find solutions that will work for you without overextending or compromising yourself. What are your emotional limits—the things that will emotionally exhaust you so you're unable to perform your best? What are your ethical limits or non-negotiables? Your values play an essential role in guiding your actions.

Next, what are your executional limits? Think about what you're able to achieve within a set time frame without overextending yourself, because doing so can lead to burnout. Executional limits also apply to your capabilities and where you'll need to seek outside resources to accomplish a task.

When you know your limits, you're able to lead with more authenticity and clarify your expectations to both yourself and your team.

As I began a new season after a break from coaching, I took a completely different tactic than usual. I asked the team, "What do you need from me?"

They looked at me like I had something growing out of my ears. Then they said, "Well, we want you to be nice. We don't want you to yell at us."

"Done. What else?"

"We want to have fun."

"Done. What else?"

"You know what? We want to learn something."

I put their future in their own hands. It was a very different approach from, "I'm the coach. This is what we're doing and how we're going to do it."

Of course, as a coach, I must have non-negotiables, because that's what keeps me authentic. But I let them have some freedom. They had fun without any yelling, and they were enjoying practice and coming back. I thought they might even stay with the game a little longer because I created an environment that allowed them to make mistakes. It created a learning environment where they could take risks and learn from the results. They were safe to try new things and test boundaries, which allowed them room to grow.

Because I was confident in my ability as a coach and knew my personal limits, I was willing to open up the strategy to my team and ask questions to get the best understanding of their needs and desires. As a result, I was able to create a leadership strategy that worked for me and for them. If I'd gone in with a strict idea of what my coaching method would be and a list of rules I read in some leadership book, I wouldn't have been able to listen to their needs and provide an engaging learning experience for the team.

DISC ASSESSMENT FRAMEWORK

One of my favorite ways to develop better self-awareness is to start with a DISC self-assessment.

The DISC framework is based on the psychological research of William Moulton Marston, who identified four traits that tend to predict certain aspects of a person's behavior. While the DISC framework has been around for many years (first published in 1928), it's been used in a variety of ways. I'm a particular fan of TTI Success Insight's DISC assessment and tools, which place an emphasis on understanding people's behaviors as well as communication styles.

Understanding people's behavioral and communication styles is particularly useful for leaders. It gives you valuable information to help you adapt your approach to work with individuals whose styles are very different from yours. It also helps you determine how to address a variety of situations and place people in roles they're suited to.

The DISC assessment measures individuals in four categories:

Dominance: People with a high level of dominance tend to be task-oriented, direct in their communication, and guarded.

Influence: People with a high level of influence tend to be people-oriented and open, action-driven.

Compliance: People with a high level of compliance tend to be task-oriented but passive, preferring indirect methods of communication.

Steadiness: People with a high level of steadiness tend to be open, people-oriented, and passive, with an indirect communication style.

It's important to note that nobody falls completely into one category or another. Rather, we each have a different level of each trait, which, combined, determine much of our behavior.

I start every session with my leadership clients with DISC and use that context for our conversations, where I ask about what's going well, what their challenges are, and how I can help them navigate those. DISC helps both me and my client understand what they bring to the table and what obstacles are in the way of accomplishing a certain task.

The underlying principle of the DISC assessment that aids our conversations is communication. How and how often are they communicating with their team members? What's the tone of that communication? Is it one-directional?

The DISC assessment helps reveal how individuals deal with difficult interactions. For example, people with different DISC profiles may challenge one another and have difficulty forming harmonious relationships, even though both bring valuable skills and experience to a team. But if we don't discuss these styles, we may make misleading judgments about one another.

If you understand the DISC profile of each of those individuals, you can see where their boundaries are and where they can meet. You can change your approach to communication—how often, time of day, tone of conversation, etc. Meet them where they are. It's a little bit like a game.

DISC gives you insight into how to speak other communication languages and validate those languages. It offers methods to better facilitate communication rather than shutting each other down.

TAKEAWAYS

- Self-awareness allows you to discover why you have the skills you do, where you lead well, where you underestimate yourself, and how others respond to your attitudes and behaviors.

- Knowing yourself allows you to create your own leadership strategy that's based on your strengths rather than adopting the strategies of others that may not work as well for you and your unique situation.

- Identify your limiting beliefs—e.g., "I'm not good at that"—and look backward to discover why you believe that. What brought you to that conclusion? Reflect on a time when you had success at something relating to that belief. What made those situations different? What can you learn from it?

- Creating goals is a negotiation. New goals are not add-ons—they are exchanges.

CHAPTER 3

Grow Your Confidence

"The essence of being as good as you can be is to figure out who you are."

–Pete Carroll, in his last press conference as head coach of the Seattle Seahawks

---

When I was a teenager, I had no idea what confidence was. I was told I had confidence, and it felt like a compliment because people often say things like, "Just have confidence in yourself."

As I got older, I realized that while I may come across as confident, it was because if I did not feel comfortable in a situation or with a new task, I simply didn't do it. I'd stay within my comfort zone, doing things I'd done before or watched enough other people do, and I felt comfortable doing it myself. I can see why that might appear like confidence to some people, but it wasn't. My confidence level was directly related to how successful I thought I would be.

I didn't uncover this about myself until I was a middle-aged mother of four. "Come on, Mom, just try it!" my kids would say when I opted out of something they were doing that I didn't understand.

But the moment I stopped opting out and joined them was the single most liberating thing I have ever done.

I am still a self-professed chicken in certain scenarios—anything I perceive as dangerous—but I now understand that in order to grow and to experience my life fully, I must attempt new things with a childlike attitude: What's the worst that can happen?

In most cases, the answer is simply that I could fail. I might look foolish and feel vulnerable.

But being willing to take the risk of failure—even embarrassing failure in front of my kids—often led to the best possible outcomes. My children cherished the experiences we had together, and I gained new perspectives from the experiences. Sometimes I was even okay at whatever I was trying to do.

That's what confidence really looks like. It's the ability to step out of your comfort zone even if you might fail. And if you do fail, it's being okay with that and learning from it rather than internalizing it or identifying with it.

I think many people want to avoid any chance of failing in public—they want to keep all their failures private. But doing so holds you back from extending yourself in any public setting. You lose the opportunity to grow, to discover strengths you didn't know you had, and to learn from failure. If you don't extend yourself with the possibility of failure, you also lose the possibility of success.

Failing publicly shows your humanness and shares it in a way that others can relate to, and it opens doors—doors to better teamwork, learning opportunities, and unimaginable success and fulfillment.

CONFIDENCE COMES FROM SELF-AWARENESS

Confidence is rooted in self-awareness. Self-awareness eliminates self-doubt because you understand your strengths and where you need help. You know your realm of expertise, what you're capable of, where you need to grow, and what you need to outsource.

Understanding your realm of expertise helps you know where to draw your boundaries as a leader. I lead in the direction I'm comfortable and confident. I know where my boundaries are, and if I'm asked to work outside those boundaries, I can say that's outside my realm of expertise and look for another solution.

I'm coaching a 14-year-old student in volleyball who wants to change positions to become a back row specialist, though she's currently in the front row. So I'm taking her through the drills I know to help her develop those skills. However, I can no longer demonstrate those skills for her, so I have to bring in someone else who can. Because I'm aware that's outside my realm of expertise, I can work around it with confidence.

The same applies to leadership. When you understand your own capabilities, you know where to supplement them to be the most effective leader. Rather than questioning yourself in a situation, you'll be prepared to answer any challenges you may face because you understand your boundaries and reasoning. If you don't know the answer, you will find it. However, admitting ignorance or saying, "I don't know," can be tough for some leaders.

Self-awareness also affords you the confidence to embrace new challenges and take opportunities. If you're aware of your skills and understand the rules of the particular environment—whether that's speaking on a stage or playing a volleyball match—you have a realistic expectation of what a scenario's outcomes will be and what kind of challenges you may encounter. You have the perspective of experience to inform you what options are available and what will and won't work.

There are always multiple ways to approach a problem and some of those options are guaranteed to fail, while others may have a strong chance of succeeding. Confidence comes from living those experiences and knowing what will and won't work in a scenario. What options do you know will work, not only in your mind, but also in practice? What have you experienced? If there's an option you don't have experience with that seems to have potential, you can seek out the expertise of others to determine whether it's the right course.

Good leadership doesn't stop with understanding your realm of expertise and acting within it. You have to continue to push forward and gain knowledge in areas you're not as confident— not to fake it till you make it but to sit with the discomfort of being unfamiliar with something in order to learn.

Aha Moment

It doesn't take confidence to act within your realm of expertise–confidence is about stepping outside your comfort zone and being willing to fail in order to grow.

YOU DON'T NEED A TITLE TO LEAD

I was hired as a manager along with another woman, who was a coordinator, at a powerful, well-recognized organization and given a challenge to help solve a problem. We each approached it by examining our own strengths and how we could use them to attack the problem.

I could see from the beginning that my colleague was amazingly observant, remembered things well, and was very detail-oriented. She liked to do things by the book, but she also went in depth. She had so many excellent thoughts, but she'd never share them with the group of four on our team—she'd only share them with me individually.

In the group of four new hires, I considered all of us equals even though we had slightly different titles and pay grades. This woman was considered tier two, while another woman and I were considered tier three. My tier-three peer immediately treated our tier-two colleague as her assistant, as though she were subservient. It was disconcerting to me because they were about the same age and both excellent leaders in their own rights. But the dynamics of the situation grew worse and worse because of the tier-three coworker's air of superiority, even though none of us had worked in that particular environment before.

My tier-two colleague's confidence drifted away. It was sad to see because she'd come in so excited and confident. As her confidence eroded, her ability to ask questions in the group deteriorated as well. She'd come to me afterward and ask for my thoughts on her ideas, and I'd ask her, "Why don't you bring that up in the group?" Her answer was that our teammate would have shot it down, because she rarely let anyone finish a sentence without saying that she had a better idea.

She would never volunteer to be the first to do anything. She didn't like to fail, which crippled her even more. Her lack of confidence was affecting her work. It was disheartening to see this young woman who had so much potential be affected in such a short amount of time by a colleague who put her down.

I told her, "You have so much to offer if you build on your strengths. If there's an opportunity to take on a task that you're comfortable with, be the first in line. And if you need help, come forward and I'm there to help you, and our company has many resources you can draw from." But she continued to shrink into herself more and more as time went on.

She had many skills that the team wasn't using. I had a conversation with the director because I figured a title change might be exactly what she needed, so she was also given a tier-three title.

It changed the group dynamic, partly because of the title but also because I went to bat for her and the director supported her. It validated her, and she started to take on more meaningful work and eventually moved into an executive assistant position that was perfect for her.

HUMILITY AND EGO

Confidence is not the same as arrogance. Rather than a belief that you know everything you need to know, confidence comes from knowing yourself and knowing that there's always more to learn.

Some people simply believe they're better than others. In order for them to function, they need to think they're better, smarter, or more accomplished. And other people will react to that like it's true even if they don't believe it's true.

It's a type of leadership that can come across as being confident but is really the complete opposite—it's an internal fragility that makes the leader feel the need to boost their own self-image and uphold their positional status.

Good leaders are willing to have empathy and look at themselves with a critical eye to determine how they can improve. Even if you've messed up in the past or you've treated people badly because of your ego, you can still recover and become more empathetic and authentic.

Those types of leaders, however, aren't willing to seek out coaching—they're the type who will only be coached because they've been forced into it, and they're typically very resistant to change.

BUILDING CONFIDENCE

Now that we've discussed what confidence looks like and how it's beneficial to leaders, how do you go about growing your confidence? Everyone wants to feel more confident in themselves, and it's a journey that continues throughout your life as there will always be areas where you can become more confident. But it's especially important for leaders to develop confidence in their areas of expertise and in situations they regularly encounter. Even more critical is the confidence to do things that feel uncomfortable or may lead to failure, because that's where growth begins.

Start with reexamining past experiences and asking yourself, "What do I know, and what do I know well?" If you're faced with a particular challenge and don't feel confident in your ability to handle it, ask yourself what you've experienced before that related to this problem. What skills did you use to solve it? Is this something that's within your realm of expertise, or do you need to seek outside resources or assistance?

Next, read critically to expand your knowledge. With more knowledge comes better confidence. In a way, reading is a bit like gaining experience because it allows you to learn from other people's experiences. Of course, that doesn't mean you should simply adopt the practices that have worked for other people, but discover how the lessons apply to your own situation and skills. Read widely and critically—on topics you agree and disagree with. The more you engage with, the greater the knowledge base you'll have.

In addition to reading, ask plenty of questions. I'm always asking questions, and I encourage the people I coach to ask questions whenever they don't understand something. People who lack confidence don't ask questions because they don't want to look silly or ignorant for not knowing the answer. If you're comfortable within yourself and what you do and don't know, then you become more comfortable asking questions. It requires self-awareness and humility, the willingness to embrace your fears and to look foolish.

Be willing to ask the questions that everyone else in the room wants to ask.

Not only will you learn more, but you'll become better at asking questions, which is a critical skill for leaders. When you're confident in your ability to ask questions, you don't have to know all the answers because you know the right questions to ask to find the answers.

The most effective step for growing your confidence is to practice stepping out of your comfort zone. That means doing things that feel uncomfortable, being willing to risk embarrassing yourself and to fail, and moving forward in either case. The more you practice failing, especially failing in public, the less awkward it will feel and the less afraid of it you'll become. And if you succeed, that will lead to better confidence too. Confidence tends to have a cyclical effect and builds on itself.

The cycle begins with self-awareness. If you're aware of what comes naturally to you and what you do well, you can feel confident in those abilities. If you're intentional about how you use them, you can likely succeed.

Start by acting on what you know. Create a plan and follow through until you succeed. Success builds confidence, which will help you feel more capable of stretching yourself to reach new goals. And being confident creates new opportunities for success by encouraging you to take risks.

Ultimately, if you're intentional about your problem-solving approach, it's likely that you can succeed. Even if you don't currently have the skills to achieve your goal, if you have a plan, you can learn to evaluate your skills to see if you're in the right place to take the next step. From there, it's a matter of either taking that step or seeking the necessary information, assistance, or resources to help you develop the skills you need.

Success requires a good work ethic and the willingness to do things that feel uncomfortable, which takes confidence. And even if you don't feel confident, by pushing yourself to grow and finding small successes, you'll build that confidence as you go.

TAKEAWAYS

- Confidence is rooted in self-awareness. Self-awareness eliminates self-doubt because you understand your strengths and where you need help. You know your realm of expertise, what you're capable of, where you need to grow, and what you need to outsource.

- Good leaders are willing to have empathy and look at themselves with a critical eye to determine how they can improve. Even if you've made mistakes in the past or you've treated people badly because of your ego, you can still recover and become more empathetic and authentic.

- Grow your confidence by stepping out of your comfort zone and being willing to fail. The more you practice failing, especially failing in public, the less awkward it will feel and less afraid of it you'll become.

CHAPTER 4

Develop Your Emotional Intelligence

"All I know is that my life is better when I assume that people are doing their best. It keeps me out of judgment and lets me focus on what is, and not what should or could be."

–Brené Brown

There's much more to emotional intelligence than a warm and fuzzy feeling that helps everybody get along. It takes real work that requires breaking down your self-awareness and your awareness of others to find obstacles to communicating and leading effectively.

Those obstacles could look like a number of things. Maybe your ego is blinding you to your effect on others. Maybe you're shutting other people down by not assuming positive intent.

Emotional intelligence (EI or emotional quotient, EQ) is the awareness of self and awareness of others, and the ability to manage your emotions and influence the emotions of others. It requires empathy and the ability to observe and listen well.

Emotional intelligence is a learned skill. People aren't born with it; you have to learn it. And for many people, it's learned through early experiences and shaped during childhood, but the learning doesn't stop there. It's something you continue to develop as you learn more about yourself, meet different people, and gain more life experiences. It's also something you can actively work to improve by focusing on your self-awareness, empathy, observation skills, and mindset.

Aha Moment

Emotional intelligence can be thought of as the ability to read the room and understand your part in that room–are you influencing the room, or are you simply an observer?

When my children were small, I loved to watch them so I could catch them doing good in order to reward them. However, if they knew I was there, that changed the way they behaved—their actions weren't authentic anymore.

As an emotionally intelligent leader, I'm able to enter the room and not impart my presence or judgement—I want to observe without affecting the interaction or its content. That can be difficult to do because you may want to jump in when you have thoughts, but if you do, you won't be able to listen as well. As an observer, you can hear what's really going on, listen to pain points, and read facial expressions.

As a leader, emotional intelligence is a vital skill because it allows you to understand those you lead in order to help them reach their potential.

Emotionally intelligent leaders understand how they affect those around them and are able to adapt their approach to meet the needs of their teams, communicate more effectively, avoid and resolve conflict, and understand values and motivations that influence behavior.

Everyone already has some level of EQ, and the way each leader applies emotional intelligence looks different depending on their particular skills and experience. It's not a skill you have to learn from scratch, but rather one you can continue to develop. You already have what it takes—now it's time to draw out those skills and apply them in new ways.

Several years ago, when I was working for a larger organization, another team member asked me to coach her. I wasn't sure how serious she was about it. She had a lot of excitement and ideas in her professional work but struggled at times with follow-through, which can be a common problem for any of us.

The managing director who'd hired her was her friend, and as a result there were times when her boss ended up doing some of her job tasks on her behalf. She frequently missed days and appeared to be more inclined to talk than listen. She acted superior to the other team members because she was friends with the program director. She wouldn't let anyone even finish a sentence without cutting in and saying that she knew better. She'd be given tasks that would rarely get done until the director and others stepped in and completed them.

I was surprised when she asked me to coach her. I asked, "Are you serious about this?"

She replied, "I know that I need help because I'm new to the role, and you're a leadership coach."

Though we didn't form a formal coaching relationship, I did begin to give her feedback and professional mentorship. I don't know how much of it sunk in, because she continued relying on the director to complete her job and eventually started working from home more often, taking more sick days, and just being absent. When we did talk, I'd ask if she was listening because she never took notes. She responded, "No, I can't. I'm not really good at that kind of thing."

This individual did have strengths, but she struggled to fully embrace them—instead, she was more interested in seeking to be like others even when their methods didn't fit her needs at all, which left her frustrated. Given more time and commitment on her part, we could have worked together on helping her see the power of emotional intelligence.

If she'd grown her emotional intelligence, she would have gained confidence and been able to come into meetings with information and ideas that were more fully researched, learn to listen before speaking, become more aware of how people reacted to her, and bring more value to the conversation. Instead, she ended up looking inauthentic, trying to hijack meetings to get attention by excessive talking rather than allowing others to collaborate in the conversations.

You have to be aware of what's going on and why you're showing up in the way you are—what's the reason you feel compelled to tell a certain anecdote or to present yourself in a certain way? Is it because you want people to think you're funny? Is it because you want attention? Or does it really add value to the conversation?

DEVELOPING EMPATHY

Is empathy something you can develop? Yes! Even though it's a word we tend to associate with identity—that is, we believe someone is either an empathetic person or they're not—it absolutely can be developed, and it can help you develop your emotional intelligence and leadership skills. In fact, it's a vital ingredient to excellent leadership.

While some people may naturally have high levels of empathy, your experiences play a major role in shaping your empathy. The people you interact with and the stories you engage with create empathy.

People who read more—especially during childhood—tend to be more empathetic. And it makes sense when you stop and think about it: reading is an exercise of putting yourself in someone else's shoes, to experience something through another person or character's perspective.

Empathy is also a product of our personal experiences. I was fortunate to have experiences early in my life where I needed to be aware of others around me at all times, and this alert awareness increased my empathy and emotional intelligence.

One of the best ways to develop empathy is through curiosity. I was an incredibly curious child, which is what drove me to read so much, but that curiosity can be practiced in other ways. In Michael Sorensen's book *I Hear You*, he suggests that to develop better empathy, you should *act* curious by asking questions to understand other people and circumstances better.

Curiosity about others is the key to forming connections with them—and that's what empathy is all about. By adopting a curiosity-first attitude, you avoid snap judgments or assuming negative intent. As you practice curiosity and adopt a curious mindset, you'll learn to slow down in order to understand and empathize with others.

It's particularly important for leaders to be curious about the people they lead. The more you learn about the people you lead, the better you'll be able to empathize with, understand, and lead them. Ask them questions and learn about their backgrounds, past issues, and current challenges, then think about how you might feel in a similar situation. If you've experienced a relatable situation, recall how you felt and how you reacted.

Sorensen challenges his reader to recognize the person's humanity, their fears, hopes, uncertainties, pain, and joy. Everyone has these experiences, and even if you haven't experienced a situation similar to what someone else is going through, you can relate to the base emotions they're experiencing. Everyone is a product of their past experiences. By understanding those experiences, we can connect on a deeper level and understand each other.

One of my favorite tools for connecting with others is eye contact. I've always coached my players and children to understand the importance of eye contact because I believe it's the most powerful communication tool aside from physical contact. Have you ever locked eyes with someone you just met? The connection can feel so powerful you may feel an instinctual urge to pull away. I encourage you to resist the urge to look away, even if it feels embarrassing or silly—just hold the eye contact. Try to express emotions, then see if you can receive emotions through that connection. The initial eye contact you make with individuals is superficial. It is the extended visual connection which creates that caring bond, that sincerity that is necessary for empathy.

Eye contact is a great way to show empathy; empathetic eyes can speak volumes. When you're looking into someone's eyes, think about how they're feeling. It can be helpful to even say in your head, "I care about you. I'm curious about what's in your heart and what you're experiencing." Eye contact can take you closer to recognizing emotions, both positive and negative. When another person allows you in by sharing their emotions with you, show your appreciation by trying to understand those emotions.

As you travel further in your leadership journey and you are ready to take another leap into a deeper empathetic understanding, Sorensen suggests imagining the individuals on your team as young children in order to see their potential vulnerabilities and feel their more basic emotions.

How would you feel as a leader and a coach interacting with a child who felt fearful, shameful, or even embarrassed? What types of words would you use? Encouragement and empowerment are effective tools for leading with empathy.

When using this approach, take caution to only observe basic emotions. If you try to puzzle through someone else's deeper emotions, you're in danger of misinterpreting and assigning your own emotions to them.

Start With Self-Empathy

Like almost every other leadership skill, emotional intelligence is based in self-awareness. Although Sorensen lists this as his fourth tip, I believe it to be numero uno: learn to know and identify your own emotions.

By making a habit of paying attention to your own emotions, you'll improve your ability to recognize the emotions of others. You'll also have a better understanding of the feelings that affect your decisions and behaviors and influence the people around you.

Some people really need to hear this: "Fine" is not an emotion. Dig deeper and ask yourself how you're really feeling. It might not come easily at first, so if you find it challenging, you may need to take a step back from outside distractions and set aside time to reflect by taking a walk or creating some quiet time without any activities. It can also be helpful to name the emotions you *are* aware of when they arise.

Create a habit of checking in with yourself throughout the day. The best way to do this is to set an alarm on your phone for several times during the day with the words, "How am I feeling right now?" If you're able, write down your answer. As this practice becomes part of your daily process, it'll become easier to remember on your own. Then, when you need it, particularly when emotions lead to actions, words, or moods, checking in on what you're feeling will be almost automatic.

Understanding your own feelings allows you to take control over their trajectory. Recognize and identify them, and then decide if your emotions will dictate your actions or if it is more appropriate to control and direct them in another direction.

By practicing this, when you notice emotions coming from others, you can empathize and help direct the conversation: "I hear some emotion in what you are saying. Can you identify what you are feeling? Can I help? What would be helpful?"

From there, you can work together to move the conversation and emotion in a productive direction. Empathy is dressed as awareness—pay attention when she arrives at the ball.

Aha Moment

Empathy and judgment are mutually exclusive, and empathy should be the goal of an effective leader.

Open up your scope with curiosity, put yourself in someone else's shoes, and reserve your judgment. This goes for yourself as well. Be just as understanding and empathetic with yourself, avoiding self-judgment—you can be your own worst judge.

As important as self-awareness is, it comes with another caution: the goal is acceptance. Be aware of repressed or suppressed emotions. Are you avoiding or ignoring the emotion you are feeling? The habit of pushing down emotions to avoid feeling them can create a host of negative side effects, even ones that effect your health.

Without understanding the feelings that drive you, you cannot grow.

So if you're someone who tends to avoid feeling your emotions, it's time to begin changing that habit and instead practice acceptance.

Acceptance is a learned behavior. After all, we avoid feeling our emotions to protect ourselves from pain. But when you do that with negative feelings, your positive feelings also get dampened. Practicing self-empathy requires you to accept those feelings and allow them to affect you. If you need to make space to feel those things in private, that's okay, but don't forget to let the feelings out. Find an avenue for release, such as exercise or journaling. Review your strong feelings and find their source. When you let them go, you make room for new thoughts, feelings, and plans for the future.

Some people may find it easier to accept others' emotions more than their own, or vice versa. Acceptance needs to be practiced all around. Acceptance leads to validation. Validation leads to support, and support leads to transparent and trusting communication. This is where the significant coaching gains are made, skills are honed, and ideas are turned into principles.

Being empathetic is a skill, and skills can be learned and improved. As James Clear wrote in *Atomic Habits,* "Your habits are the engines that drive your life."

POSITIVE INTENT

One of my most valuable guiding principles for leadership is to assume positive intent. This plays a key role in empathy because it shapes the way you approach interactions with others as well as how you treat yourself.

What does it mean to assume positive intent?

When I have a critical thought about someone, how does it change the script to assume positive intent on their part? Let's say one of your team members comes into work and is fired up, marching down the hall. Your initial reaction may be that they're angry with you, but perhaps they're really excited about something. You don't know until you give them the chance to talk to you. And if you assume negative intent, you shut down whatever they were about to share. But if you assume positive intent, you open up the conversation and allow them to share what they're excited about.

I often see others assume negative intent, especially among women, though men definitely do it as well. It's easy to assume someone dislikes you or is angry with you when the reality is they're not even thinking about you. "She's mad at me, so I'm not going to talk to her." Even if that person is angry, chances are it has nothing to do with you at all.

If you're highly empathetic and easily pick up on other people's negative emotions, it can be difficult to assume positive intent. But if that's the case, it's even more important to assume positive intent. Otherwise, you can quickly spiral into negative thoughts that may be well beyond the scope of what the other person actually feels.

For example, let's say you bring up an idea at a meeting and you can tell by the look on someone's face that they don't like it. You may become emotional in reaction to thinking that person doesn't like your idea when in reality, maybe they simply didn't care or even the exact opposite—they're so engaged the look on their face seems shocked. It's easy to misread others' feelings.

Empathetic people tend to be very high in EQ, but they're also more vulnerable to feeling judged by others even when no one is judging them. But empathy and EQ are valuable skills, so to become an effective leader, you need to be able to balance the emotions you feel. You can do that by making a habit of assuming positive intent. Anytime you begin to assume judgment or negative intent from someone else, take a step back and remember that you don't know what they're thinking or feeling. Then, assume positive intent as you interact with them.

Over time, it will work like muscle memory, but you have to learn to use it regularly. It's a little bit like sports. Volleyball is a difficult game to learn, and it can be embarrassing as a beginner because it's not intuitive—everything is the opposite of almost every other sport, pushing the ball away rather than trying to catch it. If you want to get better, until you develop the necessary muscle memory, you have to be aware of everything you're doing. It's helpful to break things down to the elemental level, pause, and take smaller steps until the practice becomes rote.

To create a habit of assuming positive intent, recognize the situations where you need to assume positive intent, then practice it. The more aware of it you are, the easier it will become.

While your standard practice should be to operate under the assumption of positive intent, that only stands until it's proven wrong. Assuming the best of others does leave you open to some vulnerability because you're trusting others. If someone proves to have negative intent, your approach may need to change. However, it's critical to interrogate whether what you're interpreting as negative intent truly is that, or if it's simply a result of something you don't yet understand. Stay curious about others. Remember to ask questions, and do so nonconfrontationally, assuming positive intent until proven wrong.

Assuming positive intent among your team can be a risk, but it's necessary in order to empower them to take responsibility for their own work. If you assume negative intent, you'll always be on edge and you'll begin to micromanage them. "Did you get it done? I know you're not going to do it."

When you make a habit of assuming positive intent, you'll be less anxious and less susceptible to micromanaging, assuming that others will do what's needed. When you believe that, you can go on with your own work and act as if it's true, which allows you to focus. There's always the possibility that you'll be wrong and that someone will drop the ball, but if assuming positive intent is part of your modus operandi and part of your daily interactions, you'll build trust with your team and they will be more likely to try to live up to your assumptions and expectations of them.

TAKEAWAYS

- One of the best ways to develop empathy is through curiosity. As you practice curiosity and adopt a curious mindset, you'll learn to slow down in order to understand and empathize with others.

- Developing emotional intelligence starts with understanding your own feelings better. Remember that "fine" is not an emotion. Dig deeper and ask yourself how you're really feeling.

- Always begin by assuming positive intent. It shapes the way you interact with others and builds trust with your team.

CHAPTER 5

Stepping Out of Your Comfort Zone

"Don't permit fear of failure to prevent effort. We are all imperfect and will fail on occasions, but fear of failure is the greatest failure of all."

–John Wooden

━━━━━━━━━━

When I was hired as development director for a small nonprofit, I was well into my personal journey as a leader. In my interview for the position, I was open and authentic in expressing this to the hiring board. "This is a nice change," they said. "You are just what we have been needing." In the months following my hiring, things clicked. The board was very supportive of the skills, personality, and enthusiasm I brought not only to the role but to the organization itself. It appeared to be a win-win.

The current executive director was retiring, and he and the board were interested in me assuming his role. So six months into my development role, I was promoted to executive director. This was a terrific show of confidence from the board members, and by this time they had a very good idea of my leadership style.

The first year was a success. I brought some effective innovation to the organization that helped them expand their service to the community. However, I could sense some rumbling at the board meetings. As I presented new or bigger steps outside of what had always been done, the support seemed less enthusiastic and more hesitant. After about 14 months from my original hire, I began to hear things like, "But we've never done it that way. Let's do it the way we have in the past."

These can be dangerous and deadly words to a new leader, but this particular board was determined to stay their course. Even though we'd raised more money than ever before through an event I had planned and we had executed very differently from past events, the board wanted to pivot and return to the old way of operating. They felt threatened by stretching their comfort zone and didn't want to expend the energy to adjust it. I chose to step away from the role and allow them to revert. It was no longer a match. Even though the board thought they wanted change, the truth was they were comfortable with status quo. And although I was confident in my leadership path and could see places to stretch the organization, the board was not ready.

Growing your leadership abilities doesn't stop with looking back or looking inward. You have to take what you've learned from examining yourself and apply it to continually improve. But growth doesn't happen inside your comfort zone—it requires a little discomfort.

You gain from new experiences. They pull you forward. They push you to succeed in new ways and help you build confidence by trusting in your instincts and experiences.

You have to stretch yourself in order to make progress. Sometimes we don't leave our comfort zones and step into the unknown simply because we haven't discovered the other options out there, but often it's because we're afraid of failing, looking foolish, or feeling vulnerable. But trying new things is necessary to build confidence.

If you've paid attention to your past experiences, remembering past successes can help propel you out of your comfort zone. When you're confident in what you know, it becomes easier to take the chance that you might fail because you have other skills to fall back on. But it's also a powerful practice to remember past failures. When in your experience have you pushed through failure and challenges and had greater rewards as a result?

THE IMPORTANCE OF VULNERABILITY

In order to step out of your comfort zone, you have to be okay with some level of vulnerability. Vulnerability is the opposite of the ego, and it's necessary for effective leadership.

When I first started coaching, I felt that I needed to know everything and what I said should be the end-all. But when I coached at my first camp, I realized just how little I knew and had to swallow my pride. I had a mindset that what I was bringing to the students was more important than what they brought to me, but that script quickly flipped as I began to realize how much I could learn from them. That required vulnerability to admit, even to myself, that I needed to learn from them.

In the camps I put on early in my career, some girls didn't seem to want to be there, and I thought they weren't even trying. Because I assumed their reasons for being there were not in alignment with mine, I didn't try to coach them up. Instead, I just focused on the kids I thought were there for the right reasons.

At one point, I said something almost mocking to one of the girls at that camp, and when I did, it hit me like a ton of bricks. That moment has stuck with me for over 30 years. I wasn't there to push my agenda but to support the students, and I had failed because of my invulnerable attitude. Many leaders are just in the room to push their own agenda, but I had to admit that I'd done a terrible thing in order to grow.

Aha Moment

Living with vulnerability means that you understand you don't know everything. Your ego is gone, and you don't feel like you need to have all the answers.

The first time I saw the leaders in my life—coaches, parents, etc.—show vulnerability, it was always an eye-opening moment that changed the way I viewed our relationship. It made me respect them more as leaders. Authority alone doesn't give you a good reason to respect someone. It doubles your respect when a leader becomes approachable and human, because you're better able to connect with them.

PERFORMANCE PRESSURE

My life has been blessed in many ways, including natural athletic ability, which has allowed me to experience success in many athletic pursuits. However, my family taught me from a very early age to avoid failure. My father didn't see failure as an option, let alone a learning tool. This stunted my growth as an athlete, a leader, and a human being. I steered clear of things I didn't know I'd succeed at immediately. As a youngster, I took few chances in order to prevent myself from what I perceived would be public humility if I failed.

Most of us learn early on that people are watching us, even though that's usually not the case. People don't care as much as we tend to think they do. But when you feel watched, it changes how you approach things. It's often better to create a mental vacuum where you focus on doing what needs to be done rather than worrying about what other people are thinking about you.

I experienced the pressure of being watched as an athlete, especially in high school. And as a coach, plenty of my athletes struggled with it as well. When I coached teenage girls, it would change their performance if their boyfriend attended the game. Whether that change was a good or bad thing varied—they could fail because they felt nervous or they could shine because they had someone they cared about watching them. The difference often came down to whether they assumed positive intent, knowing that someone was there to support them and wanted them to be successful.

The same goes with any kind of audience. Pitchers deal with a lot of pressure. In fast-pitch softball, the team will fail without a good pitcher. If I'm a pitcher and I look at the audience and think they want me to fail, that's heavy. But the reality is that nobody wants to watch a game where the pitcher is terrible—they want to watch her succeed. I try to instill the mindset in my players that the audience is there to support them, and it flips the script.

People have a tendency to think that others are watching and judging them. But in most cases, they're not. And when you assume positive intent, you can remove that feeling of being in a fishbowl.

Approach New Tasks With a Strategy

When it comes to trying new things, it can be helpful to build some momentum by setting yourself up for a greater chance of success. My strategy is to develop bite-sized tasks that have a very high success rate, something small that you can easily win. Each of those bite-sized tasks adds up to something much larger, and then you simply have to put the pieces together.

I've done this many times with my athletes on the sports field. If I'm coaching softball, I'll start with one skill and build from there—if you don't know how to run from home plate to first base, it won't do you any good to hit the ball. We break down the skills into smaller tasks where they can succeed more easily.

The same goes in a working environment. Let's say you're trying to improve your conflict management skills and want to learn how to lead effective critical conversations where you address your criticisms to a team member. In that situation, you can't just flood them with all of your complaints—you have to build up to it, and it's often more successful if you break it down into smaller pieces that allow you to focus on one thing at a time. From there, you can have a series of conversations and elevate each one. Not only is it easier for you as a leader, but it's also easier for the person you're coaching to take in that feedback.

This sounds simple, but it does require practice and intentionality. When you run into an obstacle to your progress, it's easy to get tripped up and simply stay where you are rather than try something new or develop your skills.

REDEFINE FAILURE

One of the biggest challenges to stepping out of your comfort zone and growing your leadership abilities is often the fear of failure. And when you're leading others, it's difficult to fail privately, since your actions affect the people you lead.

Many of us want to take the chance to fail in private, holding us back from taking risks in more public settings. But failing publicly can actually be beneficial. It emphasizes our shared humanity and can open doors to teamwork, learning, and new opportunities for success.

You can gain some power over failure, and your fear of it, by redefining it. What does failure mean to you? Look back on your experiences of failure in the past. What made those experiences failures? Was it that you didn't achieve your goal in that particular scenario? If so, it was a failure to achieve the goal you set. You can redefine that by reexamining your goals—maybe you need to look at different goals.

Of course, this method won't work every time. There are times when you know you've failed. What do you do with those feelings? When I was younger, I tended to take failure very personally. It felt insurmountable until I was given an opportunity to redefine it. Redefining failure happens through a self-dialogue and asking questions. Do you want to use the word failure, or do you want to think about it differently? Maybe you just failed to hit the target that time—and the target is sometimes tiny.

Aha Moment

When you give yourself grace and open yourself to growth from failure, you turn failure into something purposeful.

I had a goal for a team I was coaching to win the district championship. I shared that goal with them from the beginning, and they looked at me like I was crazy because, at that point, we didn't even know each other's names. We struggled early in the season, losing several matches. The second half of the season was better and we won enough games to get the final seed in the tournament. We failed along the way with our metric of wins, however we gained confidence and learned from our losses. And we managed to reach the championship game of districts but didn't win, and they were okay with that. So was I. The team was successful in getting to that point. And even though we didn't reach our specific goal, we celebrated how much we had improved from the beginning of the season.

I'm a believer in visualization. When I want to achieve something, I can hear it, feel it, and smell it. Those things are part of my self-talk, but they can also make failure feel more difficult. From there, I have to take a different approach to self-talk. Were you shooting for the right thing? Was it really attainable? How can you expand the target?

Learning to redefine failure can help you prepare for failure or success from the time you take on a new endeavor. Think through questions like these: How will this impact me if I do fail? How will it impact me if I succeed? What does success look like, and how wide is that target?

Do You Fear Failure or Success?

Fear of failure is one of the most common obstacles keeping people within their comfort zones and holding them back from real growth, but sometimes the mental and emotional obstacles we face are more complex than they may seem. The possibility of success can be just as frightening as the possibility of failure. Succeeding at your goals creates change and may require you to take on more responsibility or propel you in a new direction. It might force you to grow in ways that are uncomfortable.

Sometimes the fear of trying something new is the fear that it'll take you down the wrong path, and you'll have to back up and correct it. And in some cases, it's not possible to back up. The reality is that there's no correct path or answer, but if you don't try, you won't gain anything. Trying something new isn't a yes-or-no question; it's not like calling a ball on a volleyball court out of bounds.

It's easy to feel paralyzed by the possibility of making the wrong decision and avoid the decision altogether. But in doing so, you relinquish power over that decision, and often, truthfully, there isn't a wrong answer.

Another mental obstacle can simply be avoiding the challenge or obstacle itself rather than its outcome. When your emotions are entwined with something you're trying to do, you might procrastinate it because you feel underprepared or avoid it because you know it's going to be difficult, even if you know you're capable of succeeding.

Whatever stands in the way of gaining new experiences, you must recognize that it's impossible to grow without experiencing some discomfort. People tend to be extremely good at coming up with reasons not to step out of their comfort zones. But unless you try new things and stretch yourself, your abilities will narrow by practicing only the things you know you're good at, and you'll become less effective as a person and leader. When you remain only within your comfort zone, you are less adaptable, and when new situations arise—as they inevitably do—you'll feel paralyzed.

The leader who stretches their comfort zone, tries new things, and looks for ways to grow even when it isn't comfortable is better prepared for the inevitability of problems and unexpected situations. The nature of life is that you'll always encounter new things you haven't dealt with before. If you're not afraid of failure, you'll be able to reflect on your own strengths and find the necessary skills or resources to address the situation.

TAKEAWAYS

- Growth doesn't happen inside your comfort zone. Try stepping beyond it and you will gain confidence, even when it doesn't feel perfect at first.

- Redefine failure by examining your past failures. What made those experiences failures? How did you recover from them?

- Failing publicly can actually be beneficial. It emphasizes our shared humanity and can open doors to teamwork, learning, and new opportunities for success.

- The only wrong answer is no answer at all. If you avoid making a decision, you relinquish any power you have to influence the outcome.

CHAPTER 6

Listen to Your Instincts

"Do what you feel in your heart to be right,
for you will be criticized anyway."

—Eleanor Roosevelt

When I'm asked for advice from anyone, my number one response is "Go with your gut!" Coaches and leaders make decisions based on intuition every day. It can be difficult to discern where an intuitive feeling is coming from, but the answer is usually from past experience.

If you're uncertain about a decision, you can use an exercise I call playing the ambivalence. Act as if you have made a decision and notice how it feels. Play it out as long as necessary—a few minutes, hours, or even days. I learned this trick when I was 24 and trying to decide between two jobs—a promotion at my current workplace, a sales and catering manager position at a Holiday Inn, and a position for the head volleyball and softball coach at a local college.

While weighing decisions, the idea is to act as if you have made the decision and pay attention to how it feels. If you have the luxury of time, play it out for a week or even just a few days. Sometimes a few hours or a matter of minutes is enough. The key is to know yourself and be in touch with your intuition.

After a week of playing the ambivalence, imagining I had taken the hotel job, I realized I would be missing out on an early opportunity to coach and build my skills by taking the promotion. So at 24, I took the college coaching job heading up an NAIA-affiliated volleyball team in the fall and softball team in the spring. On average, I was only three and a half years older than my players, and some just a matter of two years, but based on my recent playing and graduate coaching experience, I thought I was prepared.

It's also important to establish the risk involved and seek data to support your decisions. Then evaluate whether the situation warrants the risk. Leaders must identify risk and weigh it against all the other factors affected: people, time, tools, and even the legacy of the team or organization. This is why I like to play the ambivalence for as long as possible in order to give myself time to evaluate risks and gather data.

Aha Moment

Whatever decision you make, believing that you are making a good decision will create a better opportunity for those you're leading to support the path you've chosen.

Own the decision and ask those you're leading to take action on it. And if it fails, take responsibility. Leaders have to be strong in their core convictions.

In one regional softball tournament, I knew my team's success would rely on whether or not I made a pitching change in the final inning. Based purely on a hunch, I did not make the pitching change. When we took the field for that last defensive stand, I talked with my pitcher and she was ready to close out the game with the one-run lead we had. I left my pitcher in and the next batter hit the ball over the fence for a homerun. Bummer.

Instantly I felt the heat and heard the queries: "Why didn't Coach make a pitching change? That pitcher looked tired. I would have taken her out."

It was a decision I made and it didn't work out. The loss was heavy and as a coach you sometimes protect your players from the burden. I was willing to carry it so they didn't have to.

Consider your leadership decisions as much as possible. Is there a way to ease in, or is it like a mid-inning pitching change? Sometimes you have to make a quick decision and it doesn't always work out. You will learn from it and your team members may learn from it. Do not allow it to derail you. Leadership requires decisions; how you respond is where the real lesson begins.

Listen, recall, learn, reflect, and leap!

"The only real valuable thing is intuition."

–Albert Einstein

LEARNING TO TRUST YOUR INSTINCTS

Instincts or "gut feelings" are a product of past experiences and are often a result of your subconscious noticing things. Humans are capable of making complex calculations in our heads remarkably quickly, especially when it comes to social situations, and part of how we're able to do that is through the power of the subconscious.

Your subconscious is constantly picking up on details you're not consciously aware of and interpreting them into thoughts and feelings you *are* aware of, allowing you to make decisions extremely efficiently. Sometimes you're not even aware you've made a decision until after you've already acted on it.

Think of it a little bit like driving—someone runs a red light or swerves into your lane, and before you even realize what's happening, you've maneuvered out of the way. Your conscious brain is involved, but you react so quickly that you're not having to think about what to do—most of the thinking is handled by your subconscious, which is able to predict the trajectory of the rogue vehicle, examine your surroundings, and determine the best course to keep you, the other driver, and any other vehicles around you as safe as possible. You don't have to do any physics equations on paper—you just have a feeling and you follow it, and it keeps you safe. Sometimes that feeling is wrong because there are always factors you can't predict, but more often than not, following it results in the best outcome. You have to learn to trust it.

The amazing thing is that same subconscious ability can be applied in all sorts of situations, and it's extremely useful for leaders. Sometimes you simply have a feeling about what to do in a particular situation, and even though you may not be able to point to the factors that are informing your feeling, that doesn't mean they don't exist.

Aha Moment

Your subconscious draws on your past experiences and your values to inform your intuition.

Learning to trust your instincts can be challenging. Sometimes you might not feel like your intuition is speaking to you, or maybe you even feel like you don't have a sense of intuition at all. Whether you have a strong intuitive sense or not, almost everyone can benefit from tapping into their intuition more often.

Instincts can be challenging to learn to recognize and trust, but when you learn to embrace them, it's like black and white. It makes all the difference. And when you know you can rely on your intuition, it gives you a new level of confidence.

It can be particularly difficult to recognize and trust your instincts if, like me, you were raised to ignore them in favor of following the instructions of authority. This was me. I was raised to listen to authority and operate based on what I was told, and for a long time I didn't trust my instincts because I felt I needed validation in my decisions from an outside source. This worked for most of my youth, but when I began coaching and taking on roles where I had more input, I had to learn to trust my intuition because there wasn't always someone else I could look to for validation of my decisions.

It still took a long time to learn to trust myself. One thing that helped was listening to my intuition about other people's decisions. For example, if my instincts told me something was a bad idea and I watched that bad idea play out the way I expected it would, that validated my intuition and helped me learn to trust my feelings. And as I did so, I learned to allow others to trust their instincts without judgment.

Trusting your own instincts takes some trial and error and risk-taking. Even if they're wrong, if you don't commit to following through on what your instincts are telling you, you don't learn anything.

It can take some practice to learn to listen to your intuition, and this is where self-awareness comes in. Being self-aware helps you understand why you're thinking twice about something.

Your intuition is built upon your experiences, motivations, values, and emotional intelligence.

When you're aware of what drives you, it allows you to understand when your intuition is speaking to you, and understanding where those intuitive feelings are coming from can help you learn to trust them. Spend some time with the feelings you get when your intuition is speaking to you and examine them to identify what triggered them. Often, you'll be able to trace it back to your experience.

Be aware that ego gets in the way of your intuition and can block your ability to recognize it. If you're ego-driven, your desire to protect your ego prevents you from taking risks that might result in failure. Leaders with big egos tend to prioritize looking successful over learning or progressing, and may be inclined to make decisions based on impulse rather than intuition.

While it's important to trust your instincts, impulses can lead to poor decision-making. What's the difference? Impulses are often quick responses to an emotionally laden situation, or they can be urges based on ego or desire. They're influenced by your current feelings, situation, and state of mind, and don't involve much thought. Instincts, on the other hand, are tried and true. They may also occur quickly, but they are based in personal experiences and a high level of emotional intelligence.

The time when it's most difficult to trust your intuition and discern the difference between impulses and instincts is a time of crisis—or at least a situation your brain perceives as a crisis. In the heat of the moment, it can feel like a quick decision is essential. And sometimes that's true and you do have to make a decision quickly. However, more often than not, there is time to take a step back and examine the factors at play, assess risks, and listen to your intuition.

Remember that the wrong decision is better than no decision. I told my players this all the time, "The worst decision is no decision." If you make a decision, a commitment, you can quickly identify whether it was a quality decision or not and learn from it. If you don't make a decision, one will typically be made for you and you forfeit your ability to influence the outcome. Being decisive, paying attention, and understanding the risks of a decision to the extent you can will allow you to learn earlier and more often. Learn from the outcomes. Be willing to fail, adjust and try again.

When you need to tap into your instincts, here are some helpful steps to evaluate your situation:

1. **Breathe in, then slowly breathe out.** Staying calm will allow you to think more clearly and feel your instincts without panic getting in the way.

2. **Listen more than you talk.** Ask questions. The more information you gather, the better equipped you'll be to assess risks and make a decision.

3. **Remember what grounds you.** Remind yourself of your values and motivations and how those play into the decision at hand. This can provide a great deal of confidence and clarity.

4. **Stay humble and don't take things personally.** Don't let your ego take over. It's okay to fail.

TAKEAWAYS

- Go with your gut and gain confidence even if occasionally the results are not perfect.

- If you're weighing a decision, act as if you have already made the decision and pay attention to how you respond. Give yourself time to really feel if your response signals the best answer.

- The hardest time to listen to your intuition is during a crisis. Do what you can to stay calm and grounded in order to listen to your instincts.

CHAPTER 7

Leading Through Challenges

"Things work out best for those who make
the best of how things work out."

–John Wooden

When I was hired at a college to start a women's fastball program in 2001, I was coming from coaching some very successful high schools, and I was excited about the opportunity. However the 9/11 attack happened that year, and the college was endowed, supported by the stock market. Funding evaporated, but I still had to find a way to bring the team, composed of mostly freshmen, to success. For our first trip we went to southern California, and my goal was to simply test the waters to see what the competition was like—my team might either struggle or succeed.

The trip felt like a disaster from the start. We planned to fly, which was crazy at the time because of the new travel security measures in place and the fact that I had 20 students to account for. On top of that, I forgot to book transportation to the airport from the college until two days before the trip, so we ended up renting a yellow school bus. The students were packed in there like sardines with all their gear.

We got there and played, but the first game of our extended trip was pretty eye-opening. The team was beaten badly by the competition. Spirits were low on the trip back. I knew it was a pivotal moment in my leadership journey, and I needed to reframe the trip to them as a success—it helped us learn where we were in the scope of the competition and where we needed to be. It gave us an opportunity to ask, "How are we going to face these kinds of teams going forward?"

Reframing the experience for them was a challenge. I wasn't hard on the kids by telling them they should have performed better. I knew we were out of our league and I needed to keep them motivated, so my strategy was to focus on the individuals.

At a challenging time, you need to focus on the granular level because each person experiences that challenge differently and has individual needs.

In my case, some of my athletes could play at the competition's level, but we didn't have the pitchers who could allow the team to compete.

Next, I needed to find things to celebrate. I knew we weren't going to have a winning season, so what did the players want to get out of it? Finally, I had to manage expectations. I asked, "What are we really capable of doing?" It was a matter of focusing on what we *could* achieve. As a result of this approach, we had a lot of successes individually—stealing a base, making a great catch, making an excellent play, etc.

By changing the focus of my team, I was able to lead them through a challenging situation. Remember that the behavior and mentality you adopt will be mirrored back to you through the people you lead. What are you reflecting?

Understanding that your team acts like a mirror can also be a valuable tool in discovering problems in your own leadership methods. If your team is a reflection of you, they can point out things you may not realize about your leadership. If everyone seems to have a bad attitude one day, chances are they're reflecting your attitude. This is especially valuable to be cognizant of when navigating difficult circumstances.

Aha Moment

As a leader, you must be a master of intent; your team members are masters of interpretation. Match your intent to what you want your team to interpret.

Your attitude plays a huge role in the attitude of the team and can dictate their morale and willingness to bring their best selves to the table even during challenges. One of my favorite tools to use is humor. Being able to see the humor in what may appear to be a bad situation can make all the difference. It requires humility and the ability to laugh at yourself. A sense of humor also supports your own ability to lead, because it can help you remain vulnerable and humble during challenging situations, especially when it feels as though you're not in control. It allows you to keep in touch with the human side of things and allow for falls, fears, and failure, all of which are part of the human experience and necessary for growth.

Keep a sense of humor and be able to laugh at yourself, but remember that it's often best not to let the people you're leading see you sweat. Sometimes it's appropriate to be vulnerable in that way, but because your team mirrors you, if you waver, especially during difficult times, they're likely to do the same.

RESPONDING TO PUSHBACK

Sometimes you get pushback from the people you're leading, and that too is often a reflection of your leadership. Many leaders respond to pushback by becoming more rigid, but in doing so, they often exacerbate the problem as their team becomes equally as rigid in response. When you're getting pushback, it's time to go back to my favorite question: why?

Why is this person not respecting me? Is there another way they want to approach this task or situation? If they're pushing back, chances are there's a reason. There are many things that can be at play, including personal reasons, but giving them a chance to voice those helps you earn their respect and gives you valuable information to move forward. So I'll ask them why with an attitude of curiosity rather than accusation and give them the opportunity to give input. "Tell me more. I'm open to hearing your ideas. Until I have an answer to why you want to do it differently, this is the way we're going to do it."

Always make a point to hear your team out. Respect can only be cultivated when it's mutual, and that means listening to each other as adults. If you treat your team members like adults who have opinions rather than like children, you set the bar for their behavior and allow room to learn on both sides. But if you treat those you're leading like children, they're going to act like children. I'm always open to others' ideas—I always want to hear their thoughts and ideas, but I make it clear that just because I've heard them out doesn't mean we're going to do it, even though I will give it full consideration.

Let Them Stumble

It's easier when you have a good sense of humor to allow the people you're leading to be human too, to fall, fail, and feel afraid. And you need to make room for those things where they can process them safely. If you don't allow people to be human, to fail and to work through their fear, they will not be as willing to take risks because they fear the consequences of failure. So when they inevitably stumble, that's your chance to help them learn from it and move on rather than internalizing that failure. If you lead them with patience and mentor and help them put on their cape to find their superpower, they'll go much further.

COMMUNICATE THROUGH CHALLENGES

When you're leading people through a difficult situation, focus on how you're communicating. This is when I like to go back to the DISC assessment to find tools for communication and understand the best way for each person to receive information. Also ask others for their preferred methods of communication.

I worked with a woman who was a supervisor for her company and had been trying to convince her boss to purchase some sorely needed software. She'd done all the research on it and had many other people in her company in support of her. When she asked him about it, his immediate response was no. She and his direct supervisor couldn't figure out why he was saying no, and she began to internalize his response. She thought it had something to do with her personally.

His supervisor recommended that she create a breakdown of the cost and benefits of the software. She did so and sent it to the boss in an email, and his response came back, "Who is saying no to this?" He didn't even connect her verbal request with the request supported by data through email. The right type of communication changed everything in this case.

In talking with her about how this happened, I pointed out that she'd learned something valuable about how to communicate with him. He's a busy man, and I didn't think it had anything to do with her, but only with how he needed the information presented to absorb it. Regardless of why he didn't listen to her the first time, she now knows how to connect with him in the future: be slower, more methodical, accompanied by supporting information, and in writing when possible. Then, we worked on different ways to sell this boss on anything she needs.

The best way to find out how anyone wants to be communicated with is to ask them. If this boss had explained how he preferred to be communicated with, she could have avoided quite a headache.

As a leader, you need ownership of and commitment to what you've asked for. If you tell someone you want a report typed out in 72-point font on colored paper, when they submit it that way you better own that because you asked for it. Also keep in mind that sometimes people don't understand their own communication preferences, which is where tools like the DISC assessment can be particularly helpful by providing a way to examine communication styles.

Communication is especially important during challenges of any nature, from a company crisis to personal life circumstances or even when you're challenging someone to try something they haven't done before. When difficult situations arise, the need for communication grows because there's more risk involved in lack of communication or inefficient communication.

Whether you're facing challenges as a company or you know someone is going through a difficult personal situation, check in to see how they're doing, get feedback, and offer support.

When I'm leading through challenges, I stop to ask my team members these questions:

1. What's going well?

2. What has been challenging?

3. What help can I provide?

LEADING THROUGH FEAR

I am a self-professed chicken. From early in my life, when I doubted my ability to master something on the first try, I simply passed on the opportunity. I am not sure which negatively motivated me more: the fear of failing or the fear of looking foolish trying something I hadn't mastered.

I would watch from the outside and feel tinges of envy for those who could seemingly cast aside their fears and jump into an activity, like joining a conga line. I wanted to be able to act freely, to dance without fear of judgment, but I hesitated because of my fear of judgment.

It took me many years to embrace the fear and be willing to show my vulnerability. Eventually I began to regret not taking more chances. But in order to find my bravery, I had to put aside my ego and actually try something new.

Achievement meant a great deal to me, and in order to overcome the fear of looking foolish, I first had to discover that my greatest achievements tended to result from the greatest risks.

Risk management became a cornerstone for my coaching practice, and I learned to challenge my team in the same way I had to challenge myself. I reminded them everyone wants to succeed, and failure is painful for most people. But the reality is that others are generally rooting for you to succeed as well. For example, when someone is singing in a public arena, you want them to successfully hit each note—it's awkward to hear them miss and make everyone cringe. With the exception of certain types of entertainment, like car races and boxing matches, people generally want to witness others succeed, especially when it involves overcoming risks and fear. They like rooting for an underdog. Overcoming conflict is inherent to the structure of every story for this reason—it's compelling to us.

When you understand that others are likely rooting for you, it's easier to face your fears. But it requires you to look in the mirror and ask yourself exactly what you're afraid of. What does success look like to you? What are your goals? And what is keeping you from them?

Fear can push you to success, but only if you know your destination. Otherwise it simply keeps a log of the challenges and self-defeating beliefs that keep you from taking risks in the first place and undermine your achievements.

Those you lead should know and trust that you truly believe in failing as a teacher.

Aha Moment

Failing can be the motivation to achieve greatness.

For my athletes, this might look like understanding how many times they needed to practice their tennis serve—they'd fail many times before seeing and feeling success. In a tennis serve, being close doesn't count—you must hit the ball within the service area. They had to reach a point of feeling confidence in the thousands of times they'd practiced, the repetition of failing and trying again. And through those successes and failures, they could map out their comfort zone and learn where they could work to expand it.

However, when you stretch yourself out of your comfort zone, you become more vulnerable than when you stick with the tried and true. You leave yourself open for judgment and failure.

This is why it's so important to create a safe and supported space for your team to fail. That might require redefining both failure and success, so your team understands that failure is part of success. But your team needs to agree on what that looks like. How much discrepancy are you willing to tolerate, and for how long? How much room do they have in which to fail?

Self-doubt is normal, and it's okay. No one feels entirely confident in all their decisions and abilities. But you must follow that doubt to its edges, and find branches where you are confident—your skills, your values, your personality and leadership style. Ask yourself questions to determine your goals and what success looks like to you. Then, when you understand where you want to go, the shape of your comfort zone and what lies outside that comfort zone, you can begin to gain the knowledge and practice you need to move toward your goals. Expand your awareness and sphere of competency.

Information is your ticket and leading others is your vessel. They need to get on board so you can move forward together. If and when you step out of your lane, you enter learning mode again. That's not a bad step—it simply means it's time to commit yourself to expanding your field of excellence.

"Consistency is harder when no one is clapping for you. You must clap for yourself during those times. You should always be your biggest fan."

–Anonymous

TAKEAWAYS

- Your team is a mirror. They will reflect your behavior and attitude back to you.

- Reframe failure and challenges to focus on what can be celebrated.

- In challenging situations, you can't lead with a big-picture mindset. You have to approach leadership on a granular level, paying attention to the experience of each person on your team.

- Ask questions to check in on how each person is doing and how you can support them.

- Communication becomes more valuable during challenges. Ask others for their communication preferences.

- Fear can push you to success if you know your destination. Remember that others are generally rooting for you–you just have to trust yourself and be willing to take a risk and step out of your comfort zone.

CHAPTER 8

Influencing Versus Leading

"To lead people, walk beside them . . . As for the best leaders, the people do not notice their existence . . . When the best leader's work is done the people say, 'We did it ourselves!'"

–Lao Tzu

We live in a culture of influencers—a word that's often used for social media. Influencers are people who want you to follow along with what they do, to model your own life off of their lives. Unfortunately, this is a model that many leaders have also adopted.

A leader with an influencer style approaches leadership by saying, "This is what I do, so this is what you should do." They often have an agenda, and they're working from a template. An influencer might say, "I want you to read this book, which contains the secret sauce. It works for me and it'll work for you too."

This style of leadership reminds me of advertisements on late night TV—"Buy it now. But wait, there's more! Buy now and you'll get two!" They're selling something, even to the people they're leading.

Leading is not the same thing as influencing, although many leaders get this confused. Effective leaders are empowering, and they bring out the best in you. They listen. They can articulate things that resonate with individuals. Influencers, on the other hand, come into a situation with an agenda and a script and tell you what they believe in and what you're going to do.

Leaders are agile enough to adapt their presentation to the individual or the situation. They're willing to switch gears, ask questions, identify needs, and craft solutions.

It's your job as a leader to empower. If you're leading a group who is fairly inexperienced and doesn't have the capability yet to make decisions on their own, there's usually room to take on a more influencing approach in the short term. Tell them what they're going to do, but this must be done with the knowledge that when they've developed enough, they'll be able to make their own decisions because they have gained confidence and a whole new set of tools.

Leading allows those who are following to create their own path. Influencing is prescriptive and influencers often claim to have a magic pill, but their methods tend to be trendy and are usually much less effective than leading.

And influencing can be valuable. For example, I find Michael Jordan to be very inspiring, and he influences me to want to be a better leader. But I can't simply follow all of his methods and assume that they'll work for me. Influencers can be excellent at inspiring, but they aren't great at getting real results on an individual level.

Leading and influencing aren't mutually exclusive. It's possible to be an influencer and not a leader, but it's not possible to be a leader without also influencing those you lead.

A good leader doesn't try to influence others to do things the same way they do. They allow you to do you. They allow ownership and accountability. Each person on a team has different desires and needs in how they communicate, how they work, and how they want to be recognized. In order to adapt your leadership to fit well with the people you're leading, you need to know each one personally. Leaders are more cognizant of how their actions will impact others because they're tuned in on an individual level. And as a result, they're better equipped to handle challenges and to find opportunities to help their teams grow.

Aha Moment

The difference between influencers and leaders is in the delivery of their messages. Influencers sell. Leaders empower–they bring out the best in you. They listen.

Influencing is also more ego-driven. It says, "Look what I've done. I've influenced my team to do this." But a good leader gives the credit to the team. They may have given the team the tools they needed, but they recognize the credit belongs with the individuals on the team.

Leadership and influence are not black and white, but I see many people in leadership roles trying to influence rather than lead. Sometimes it's for their own gain—if they get enough people to buy into something, it'll make them feel good, so they get to say, "Look what I've done."

I find very few places in life where ego is effective or helpful. In a leadership situation, ego doesn't really have a place beyond the ability to step in and make a decision when it's needed. Ego is self-serving and reduces emotional intelligence because it's self-focused. It motivates you to serve and protect yourself over serving others. I've seen that self-centered motivation in other coaches and in a lot of umpires. When someone has a big ego, it arrives before they do, and you can feel it—it's running the show.

Everyone has an ego to a certain extent, so be aware of how yours is influencing you. A leader who is particularly ego-driven will be more inclined to influence those they lead rather than truly leading or mentoring them.

Many leaders try to lead as influencers because that's all they know. They've learned about leadership from other influencer-style leaders. That can be because they're getting their knowledge from books, online courses, and social media or because that's how they've been taught by other leaders in their organization, who may require their leaders to follow a template. They teach the answers to specific questions until they're ingrained.

Influencing tends to be more distanced than leading, and operates in a bigger sphere, where leading is more personal. It's common for influencers to use group-speak as a tool to get everyone on the same page—you've likely seen companies that share some kind of common language without much real meaning behind it. Group-speak can take the form of commonly used words, some kind of group mantra or chant, or even core values that are emphasized but mean little to the individuals on the team.

If you've learned leadership from influencer-style leaders or have been taught a template approach, learning to adapt your leadership to the needs of individuals can be difficult, especially if you're in an environment that doesn't allow you room to move or adapt. But even such limiting roles can teach you something as you learn what you *don't* want to do. How many times have you walked away from a bad job or a bad leader with a bundle of lessons, knowing how you'd like to do better and seeing more possibilities for your own development? Personally, I've had this experience many times.

Much of my own growth in leadership has come from identifying the leadership practices of others that haven't worked— and influencer-style leadership is one of those for me. While it may work for some people, it will ultimately fail to reach every individual on a team, and it can never get an organization as far as a leader who is willing to adapt their methods to the individuals they're leading and take on mentorship in addition to their leadership role.

MENTORSHIP

The best coaches are those who combine leadership with mentorship. Mentorship provides examples of success along with personalized encouragement and feedback. The best mentors share genuine praise and still challenge you to do your best based on what you know and the tools you have.

Mentorship is very distinct from influencer-style leadership. Influencing, leading, and mentoring overlap to some extent, so there are influencer-style leaders and mentor-style leaders. There are also influencer-mentors, but these people are not leaders. While many business leaders can get away with influencer-style leadership, mentor-style leadership is particularly important for coaches. Mentor-leaders can create much more impactful results than influencer-leaders because mentorship is based on a personal relationship between mentor and mentee.

Just as mentorship helps those you're leading, it's also part of your own growth. It's an excellent tool to help you understand your leadership style and build upon it, and I highly recommend seeking mentorship whenever you have the opportunity. However, sometimes you're put in a role where you don't have mentorship, and you can find it by observing a variety of other people, reading books, taking master classes online, and using other resources. I've learned from reading and observing and it has taught me a lot of self-sufficiency.

A good mentor has the mentee's best interests at heart and doesn't dictate how to do something, but gives their mentee the tools they need to do it their own way. A good mentor wants you to learn and shows what has been successful for them. To learn about what they do and where their success comes from, watch and listen. It is then up to you what aspects you adopt as your own.

The best mentors know how to ask effective questions to get to the root of an issue. Questions are necessary to get people to make change, and an effective leader has to ask "why" questions. Why are you doing what you're doing? Is it only because this is the way you've always done it? The majority of the nonprofits I've worked for use that answer for everything. "We've always done it this way, so why would we change it?"

You can't necessarily mentor the content of what's happening on your teams, but you can mentor the individuals and ask why. For example, I might have someone under me in the IT space, and I don't have any idea how their job works, so I can't mentor them in that way. But what I can do is mentor their ability to ask and answer their why questions.

It's not reasonable for leaders to understand every aspect of how to do a job, but you don't need to carry that on your shoulders. Instead, ask "What's your system?" You can ask the IT person, "Tell me about your system, and are you agile enough to get input from other areas?"

I love to hear the sentence, "I've never thought about that," because it lets me know they're thinking on a different path.

TAKEAWAYS

- Influencers sell. Leaders empower. A good leader doesn't try to influence others to do things the same way they do. They allow ownership and accountability.

- The best mentors share genuine praise and still challenge you to do your best based on what you know and the tools you have.

- As a leader and a mentor, the most powerful tool you have is questions. Start by asking why.

CHAPTER 9

Leadership Agility

"We cannot become what we need by remaining what we are. Change is inevitable. Growth is optional."

–John C. Maxwell

Every situation in leadership is unique, involving unique individuals and circumstances that a leader must consider. Leading effectively requires agility, especially since factors are constantly changing and require you to change your approach to match.

The easiest place to see the need for agility is in the way that developing technologies have made it necessary for businesses to adapt. The more inflexible leaders, who are unwilling to consider change until they're forced to make it, tend to lead their businesses toward failure by falling behind those businesses with more agile leadership who adapted their approach. And the most agile leaders are the ones who lead the way, who take risks and explore new options.

On a more everyday level, agility in leadership is all about handling things uniquely. You can't always put a template over a situation, especially when things are challenging. Instead, you have to adapt your approach to your current circumstances, think creatively, and take risks. Agility leads to resilience too in that it gives you the ability to stop and back up after a risk doesn't pan out by making adjustments and trying again.

Aha Moment

Agility is in the moment, having the flexibility to change in small iterations, constantly touching base with those you're leading and making whatever adjustments are needed.

An agile leader doesn't panic when the unexpected happens or when a risk doesn't pan out. Instead, they're able to see options when others can't. They're prepared for different outcomes in case things radically change. The agile leader isn't necessarily always changing—agility simply means having the ability to change direction.

If you're an agile athlete, you can pivot quickly. You can look at a situation and understand how to adapt to it. If you hit a wall, you have to figure out a way to get around it. In the business world, there are always situations that can be improved upon. An agile leader is able to pivot—you don't necessarily have to stay where you pivot, but you can make decisions from a new position and pivot again if necessary. If you're not able to pivot again and again, atrophy will set in.

Author Adam Grant acknowledges the value of agility in both personal and professional contexts. Being agile, in his view, involves a willingness to learn, adapt, and embrace change. It's about cultivating a mindset that is open to new ideas, feedback, and continuous improvement. In his book *Originals*, he presents agility as a foundational element of the creative process, allowing individuals to navigate challenges, pivot when necessary, and continuously evolve their thinking. The book encourages readers to cultivate a mindset that is not only original in its ideas but also agile in its approach to navigating the complexities of the world.

The agile leader has the potential to take their organization far. Many small businesses have evolved into giant businesses because someone had a vision and asked questions like "Have you thought about this?" or "What other ways have you seen that work?"

The agile leader is able to create willingness in those they lead to adapt by asking the right questions. Offering the right question can change the whole conversation. When a leader asks questions rather than telling people what to do, it communicates that they have the confidence and willingness to empower their people to accomplish whatever the answer may be.

The level of agility you need varies depending on your sphere of work, and can be particular to your industry. If you're bottling carbonated beverages, there may not be much need to be agile, because the process has to remain fairly standard. There's a difference between change for change's sake and movement for the sake of agility and adaptability. It's not only about following new trends, but being able to pivot effectively based on what's happening around you. This requires self-awareness to understand your position, as a leader, as a team, and as an organization.

The agile leader has the ability to inspire those around them to take risks and keep moving in the face of failure. Agility is contagious. It's a great starting point to exploring options. Rather than saying, "This is the way we're going to do things," I'm able to look for other options and hear ideas that stretch my comfort zone but lead me and my team in a direction of growth.

When I was a young coach, I needed to keep strict boundaries and be firm in my approach in order to keep my team from running all over me. I exerted pretty firm control over them in ways that may not have been productive. But now that I've grown as a coach, learned many lessons, and understand my leadership style and my values, I can be much more agile.

INFLEXIBLE LEADERSHIP

Leaders who are inflexible rather than agile don't allow room for growth. They may be satisfied with where they are, which isn't always a bad thing, but they don't have potential to improve. And if you're inflexible to change, it stifles your thinking.

With all the technological advances that have happened recently, I see a major difference in mindsets between generations. I'm fortunate enough to work with some younger folks who keep me on the cusp of new things that are happening, but if you don't have that perspective, it's easy to lose sight of the necessary changes the future is bringing.

Some leaders from older generations fall into the trap of being thought partners rather than agile leaders because they're comfortable in what they know. They don't always see the need to understand anything that's contrary to that because what they've always done has worked for them so far. It stifles their creativity and ultimately, people stop coming to them for input because they're unwilling to have an open dialogue about possibilities. It stifles the creativity of the team because they're unable to bring ideas and opportunities to change to their leader. Eventually, this can lead to burnout.

Coaching athletes works the same way. If they're always coached the same way, their muscles will get fatigued, and they will atrophy certain parts of their bodies that aren't being used. That's what happens with creative muscles—the ability to think creatively diminishes with a leader who doesn't adapt and allow room for creative agility. An inflexible approach to leadership feels defeating to the team, and they eventually learn that there's no point in trying to be creative. It becomes a source of frustration, which leads to burnout.

When I first began my college coaching career, I'd never played or coached softball at that level before and felt quite intimidated. I understood that I needed to have a plan to coach my team up, so I had notebooks full of thoughts, ideas, strategies, and situations. I tried to coach my first team as I had been coached in my past when I'd been playing softball.

I was determined to have more success and create a winning mentality. As the preseason began I was loaded with drills, workouts, "chalk talks," strategy sessions, nutrition plans, and mindset challenges. You name it, I had researched it and made it part of my plan for success.

We won our district title and we were headed to the national tournament with an automatic berth. The university rented two vans to accommodate all the players and gear. One of the vans overheated and stopped dead about 150 miles short of our destination, which put us about three hours behind schedule.

The first night was a banquet celebrating all the teams for their accomplishments. I had allowed time for the team to have a two-mile run prior to the banquet, but now we were three hours behind. As a rookie coach, I stuck with the game plan and told the players to take the run after they'd checked into their rooms. They were furious. "We will be late for the banquet. We can't be late."

But I insisted—not an extremely emotionally intelligent thing to do—because I was inflexible in my leadership approach. As a result, we were very late to the banquet and awkwardly took our seats in the middle of the event hall. The tension was thick and I felt very disconnected from my team. We had some wins at the national tournament and ended up sixth overall. Very respectable, and yet I can't help thinking what we could have done had I not been so insistent on doing things my way and sticking with my plan. I lacked the agility to adjust my plan for the circumstances and account for the needs of my team, and I regret that decision to this day.

AGILITY AND RESILIENCE

The crossover between agility and resilience is failure. Agility is an essential skill for leaders in all types of situations, but when it comes to failure, the ability to remain agile requires resilience.

This book is a good example of agility and resilience. Several times, I started writing and didn't finish and years went by before I came back to the project. Resiliency led me to try again. There have been so many times I have felt devastated in similar circumstances and really didn't want to push forward, such as starting a business that failed.

However, resilience can be learned. Momentum for continued successful results can be created through both positive and negative experiences. You might feel unsteady at first because you're not sure of your own resilience, but one positive tool to help you overcome uncertainty is self-talk. Tell yourself you can do this, you have seen the other side of difficulties before, and you can do it again.

Fear of failure can keep you from being agile. But resiliency tells you that you can pivot. In experiences of failure or devastation, sometimes you have to assess what you have control over. You have control over your thoughts.

Agility is about taking chances. And if you're able to recall past experiences where you found something positive on the other side of a struggle, that's a path of focus where you can see your own resiliency. If you're agile, you have the confidence and willingness to take the steps you can even in the midst of uncertainty.

Resiliency in your personal life can help you lead, but you have to approach leading differently. Each person has to come to their own decision to pivot and remain resilient. You can lead them to that point, but they have to make the decision and take the step to pivot and keep going.

It's important to acknowledge that pivoting requires some level of risk for each person, and you as a leader cannot take on all of that risk. Each person needs to take on risk for themselves, so the decision must be theirs. You can encourage it, but you can't own their risk. Whether they fail or succeed, that result belongs to them and not to you.

DEVELOPING AGILITY

Agility comes from past experience, having confidence in the skills you've learned previously to take calculated risks. It often relies on your instincts to guide you. The more self-aware you are, the easier it is to be agile because you'll be cognizant of your strengths and capabilities as well as your limitations and the fears that may be getting in your way.

Developing agility requires the ability to face the fear of failure. Taking a risk doesn't mean you have to commit to following a new path all the way through to its end—you can explore a path and pivot again when necessary. You can find your way back if you need to.

Facing your fear of failure requires you to be self-aware in order to understand based on past experience that if you do fail, you'll be okay. You can always find a new path. And even if you lead people down a path of failure, it's going to be okay because everyone is aware that you're taking a chance together.

But agility does require strong leadership skills. The good news is you already have these skills. You've already faced challenges before, taken risks, pivoted, and gone in a new direction. Draw from your internal resources, and if you need someone to help you call those resources out, go back to chapter 2 on growing your self-awareness, and seek support from mentors and peers who know you well.

Some experiences you may have had that increased agility might include parenthood, teaching, surviving middle school, going through puberty, difficult interpersonal relationships, shopping, planning logistics for a trip, scheduling, or just surviving a bad haircut. There are so many experiences throughout life that require agility—you're already incredibly capable, but you may need some encouragement. Keep your inherent agility in mind and be willing to apply it to your leadership and the situation in front of you, even if it's scary.

Aha Moment

Knowing your own leadership style is one of the best ways to stay agile. Avoid templates–they will never be as adaptable as you are.

Learn how to stretch your comfort zone, and practice doing new things for the sake of practice. Keep your team practicing agility too, and when you're planning to take a risk, evaluate where each person is on the journey to making a decision to take the necessary steps.

It's also helpful to have a lot of plans in place to help mitigate risks. A failure to plan is a plan to fail. I like to take an "if this, then that" approach to planning, and I even make plans for planning. This helps me approach the possibility of failure with an agile mindset. No matter how much planning you do, there will always be factors outside your control and sometimes the outcome just isn't up to you.

Knowing your leadership style and your own strengths and challenges helps you plan effectively, but it's not enough on its own. You must stay current with what's going on inside your field and outside of it, understanding factors that could influence your plans later on.

If you talk to people at the top of your field, you'll come to an understanding that even those who are most successful have faced many contingencies to reach their success. When observing success stories, look at people who have followed more traditional paths to success as well as rule-benders, and try to understand the reasons those paths worked. You'll discover that there are many paths to success, and the key is to stay agile while keeping your goals in mind.

When you know where you want to be as a leader and what is available to get you there, you'll have the tools to carve a path toward success, no matter how many turns you have to take along the way.

TAKEAWAYS

- Agility is contagious. The agile leader has the ability to inspire those around them to take risks and keep moving in the face of failure.

- Avoid utilizing templates–they will never be as adaptable as you are.

- Fear of failure can keep you from being agile, but resiliency tells you that you can pivot.

CHAPTER 10

The Results Are More Important Than the Credit

"The main ingredient of stardom is the rest of the team."

–John Wooden

People love to proclaim the value of teamwork, and yet many organizations claim to have strong teamwork when they don't. The word has been used so much it's lost some of its meaning. So what is teamwork, really?

Teamwork simply means that everyone is working toward the same goal. *Effective* teamwork takes more than simply sharing a goal, however.

It requires respect for each individual and the talents they bring, as well as for their unique perspective and experience. Even if there's someone new to the team who doesn't have a great deal of experience, the team still needs to hold respect for their position right now and the fact that they're learning.

Be careful not to elevate some people over others on a team, because doing so diminishes all aspects of the team. Respect starts with the leader, who must demonstrate that respect for each individual and make clear that's what's expected and acceptable within the group environment. You build a team based on respect for what each person brings and what they do. When you do, their success becomes theirs to own.

Setting expectations and ensuring each person understands the task at hand sets the team up for effective teamwork. They must know what's expected of them in order to live up to it. They also need to understand why they're a team. Why is this group of individuals working together? What pulls them together?

Trust is also an essential factor in effective teamwork. It can stem from respect, but it must be earned. While respect is a given until someone loses it, trust requires each team member to prove that they'll put in the effort, communicate clearly, and ask for help when it's needed. If you can't trust someone on your team to complete their role, you can't work effectively together.

I've always hated the phrase, "There's no 'I' in team." Many leaders focus so much on the team that they ignore the individuals who make it up, which can be detrimental. Creating a true team is combining the best of the team with the best of each individual to see what can be accomplished together. The focus isn't only on the group or only on the individual. It allows room for people to come together and perform their best individually as well. So even if they're doing something alone, they know the team is there to back them up. And there has to be an individual drive, where each person is allowed to be who they are and celebrated for that. Allowing your team to demonstrate their skills and intellect empowers the individual and lets them see how they contribute to the team.

When a team is working well together, it's an amazing dynamic that can energize each person on it. And when it's not, it's your job as the leader to slow down and figure out how to get things back on track. This job takes a leader who understands teamwork, has lived it and experienced the highs and lows, and knows just how deep it can go—but also knows how shallow it can be.

If your team is struggling to collaborate, the best way to get there is communication. It starts by ensuring that everyone understands why they're there. The dysfunction is almost always in what role they're expected to play. Often they've been assigned a role they're not suited to or there's a misunderstanding about their strengths and how their process works. In order for everyone on the team to do their best work, those expectations need to be communicated.

You want to encourage what each person brings to the team rather than siphoning people away into specific tasks, but that requires them to communicate what it is they want to bring. Sometimes that's hard—people aren't always natural communicators, and some people don't like to talk in groups. As the leader, understanding communication styles allows you to adapt to help everyone communicate well. That might mean allowing someone to write their thoughts out or meet with you one-on-one rather than voicing their thoughts in a group setting.

Expectations, goals, skill sets, and communication styles need to be established early in the relationship. Any time you onboard a new team member, they need to understand the rules of the game. That requires open dialogue—it can't follow a script, because each person is different. And that requires time and accountability.

You can create the team you want. With your drive and confidence and unique leadership style, your team will take on those characteristics and begin to mirror you.

Aha Moment

The impact you have on your team can be positive or negative–you have that power, so it's your responsibility to treat them well and give them opportunities to grow rather than putting them in a box.

A good leader will help each team member see their role within the team and understand how they can bring their best work forward and contribute. And when they do, they will exceed all expectations.

"The best leaders are those most interested in surrounding themselves with assistants and associates smarter than they are."

–Lee Iacocca

BALANCING INDIVIDUAL AND TEAM RECOGNITION

Ultimately, you want to create an environment where team members are able to take risks, step out of their comfort zones, and be rewarded for their contributions.

In most teams, some roles hold more weight or visibility and are more likely to get credit for the work of the team, while other roles may be considered supportive. The truth is that those "support" roles are just as necessary for the success of the team.

You have to balance individual and team recognition in order to maintain motivation and a sense of unity within the team, to find a way to congratulate individuals without sparking a sense of competition or resentment and to praise the team consistently.

When you give credit to an individual rather than the team as a whole, you elevate that person for something they don't really own, and you begin a mentality of keeping scores.

For example, in basketball, one player can definitely dominate the game and make a big difference for their team. It's really easy in that game to say, "You're the reason we won that game." And it's not bad to acknowledge that someone made a difference, but the impact on the rest of the team can be devastating, unless the culture of camaraderie and team chemistry is strong enough.

When giving credit in a work environment, everyone is aware of the work they've done and they all have the opportunity to contribute. Avoid singling out an individual as the reason for the team's success.

You can build up accolades to the team and then comment on the individual contributions. A good leader will be able to point those things out without sounding trite or creating an accolade that isn't really warranted. The highest priority is to acknowledge the contributions of everybody.

Then, circle back with individuals on a one-on-one basis and congratulate them or acknowledge their good work specifically. Doing so encourages them to stay more engaged in team projects.

Recognition must be part of the culture. It can't come out of the blue—it needs to happen every day. When contributions by individuals are acknowledged every day, there's no big chasm when someone is recognized for an achievement. Have conversations about culture with your team. What do we want this team or environment to look like?

The leader needs to understand who they're leading. Some people don't want recognition in a public forum. You have to understand how your team members want to be rewarded and what motivates them. That requires dialogue on an individual and a team level. Some people will say they know they've done a good job and they're happy with that. Others will say it's nice to have a pat on the back, and then you need to figure out what that means—do they want a gift card, balloons in their office, a plaque? Not everybody wants the same kind of recognition, but some people feel that they need it.

Then take it a step deeper. How do your team members feel about different forms of recognition? Do they shrink from it? Do they feel like they deserved it? You can't assume what others want based on what you want. You have to know the people you lead. Understanding what encourages and motivates them is a powerful tool, and that's where the DISC assessment comes in handy. But you have to have a dialogue, because if you miss the mark, it can do damage if you're not aware of it.

Find ways to foster intrinsic motivations because you can't give extrinsic rewards for everything. If you do, at some point they'll eventually come across as disingenuous. Instead, you want your team members to internalize their successes on both an individual and a team level. That can be challenging to do, but it comes down to rewarding what moves the organization, the team, and the individual forward.

WATCH FOR THE GOOD

One of the biggest sources of growth for me as a coach was parenting my children. For those of us who are parents, there's a great deal of overlap between that and leadership. The overlapping principle for me was to "catch them being good." When I discovered this principle, it changed something very fundamental about my parenting style. I had been raised in a discipline-focused family so it was a new concept, but it made perfect sense to me. Negative reinforcement is not my style.

Sometimes leaders are so overloaded they're only focused on what needs to be done and don't take the time to see what's happening around them or what's being done well. The premise of "catch them being good" involves looking for opportunities to praise instead of expecting the need to correct. Most people need encouragement to gain confidence. And as they gain confidence in a particular scenario or skill set, they learn that risk is a good thing because it creates opportunities for growth and success. Without the threat of negative reinforcement, they're more likely to take risks. It paves the way for constructive criticism, which is more likely to be positively received than correctional measures. They learn to trust you (the parent or the leader) to make an informed and optimistic assessment of their progress and coach them accordingly. Because they feel safe, failure can be seen as an opportunity to learn and to move on.

Leaders, like parents, want to empower those they lead to identify what success looks like and be confident enough to make changes to achieve it. Look for opportunities to catch your team members being good. If someone does something really well, they're not likely to tell you about it because it's just part of their day, even if they feel proud of it. But if someone else on the team tells you about it and you're impressed, you have the opportunity to acknowledge that person.

Aha Moment

Positive reinforcement can be a more powerful teaching tool than even constructive criticism.

Telling someone when they've done something well lets them know what the goal is and what to repeat in the future. It's more helpful to be told what to do than what not to do, because it gives you something to emulate rather than to avoid.

Make a point not to belabor criticism or failure. Move on from it, because dwelling in it and telling someone over and over to do things differently can become very destructive.

Positive reinforcement can also take the form of giving your team members your appreciation and trust. Telling them you trust them, believe in them, and are proud of them can go a long way. Chances are they don't hear those things often enough, and it will help them build confidence.

TAKEAWAYS

- Teamwork is when everyone is working toward the same goal— it doesn't matter who gets the credit.

- Each individual has different desires, and an excellent leader understands their team members well enough to know how and when to distribute credit and rewards, as well as how to balance individual and team recognition.

- Creating a true team is combining the best of the team with the best of each individual to see what can be accomplished together.

- Recognition must be part of the culture and it must be meaningful and personalized.

- Catch them being good! Positive reinforcement helps people gain confidence and teaches them what you want rather than what you don't want.

CHAPTER 11

Remember to Celebrate

"Joy comes to us in moments–ordinary moments. We risk missing out on joy when we get too busy chasing down the extraordinary."

–Brené Brown

Celebrating success is an essential aspect of leadership, because both the leader and the team need to be recognized for what they've accomplished. Celebrating accomplishments of both the team and individuals validates and creates a better sense of satisfaction while offering time to reflect and learn from the journey.

I've known some leaders who were so focused on getting to the next rung that they often forgot to celebrate when their team met a goal. This mindset is common among many high-performing leaders, coaches, and even athletes. They are so driven to reach the next mark that they don't take the time to stop and see how far they've come.

Even if you don't feel a need to celebrate or be recognized, your team needs it. Create a culture around celebrating goals that fosters a sense of success and excitement and provides opportunities to reflect on what went well and what could be improved on the journey to the next goal on the list.

Aha Moment

Celebrating successes provides validation for your goals and your process of reaching them. Celebrations also reinforce the team culture you've built.

The team and its leaders need to feel that sense of validation. If you simply move on to the next thing, you miss out on valuable aspects of celebration. It's essential for the human psyche to say, "Yes, I did this," or "We did this, and I was a part of it." There's a social aspect that makes team members feel like they belong and have contributed in a meaningful way. It can be encouraging and empowering to keep reaching new achievements, building confidence along the way.

If you don't celebrate, you create a working grind environment. You lack the endorphins that are produced when you say, "We did it!" It creates a stronger bond within the team to recognize what they've achieved together, and it can deepen your conviction as a leader to see how everyone contributed. You can celebrate while acknowledging that there's more work to be done tomorrow, but it's still a priority to pause and recognize accomplishments.

Celebration doesn't have to mean a party. It can be scaled for the accomplishment and for the preferences of those involved. But at the very least, acknowledge the achievement and take a moment to reflect. Here are some questions I like to use to guide that reflection:

1. Where have you been? Honor and celebrate this path.

2. Where are you now?

3. How did you get here? Who are the unsung heroes of this victory? Take time to remember.

When I was working for a college as a development manager for their nonprofit foundation, I was responsible for organizing events. At these events, we showcased what the students were doing. We hosted events and my team would send invitations, work with a caterer, and decorate the space.

I put on one event at the president's house where only members of a donor club were invited—it was a very exclusive event. That evening turned into a much bigger and richer conversation than anything I could have prepared for. The food was amazing, and it had been prepared by students from the culinary department, so we had the opportunity to showcase them in front of these administrative guests. Most of these students were living day-to-day—some of them living out of their cars or couch-surfing. But they were presenting in this high-class environment where they were celebrated for how they'd contributed to the event. Throughout the night, the conversation turned from the food to all about the students. They began to wonder what they could do to bolster the culinary department and help these students reach their potential.

The guests began to have conversations with the students about their aspirations, and it turned into something of a recruiting event. They made such a great impression on the guests, and it was fun and memorable. Of course, the next time we had an event, those students were more than happy to come back and do it again and top their last experience by challenging their skills.

By celebrating what they'd contributed, it elevated the entire work process. They were recognized for their achievements, and it built their confidence to move forward and challenge themselves.

CREATING A CULTURE OF CELEBRATION

Creating a culture of celebration doesn't have to be difficult, but there are a few things to keep in mind to ensure it's effective. Too much celebration can lead to diminishing returns, and not enough contributes to burnout and a sense of grinding work.

That satisfaction in a job well done is a moment of pride, but remember that you can't settle there. You have to continue to raise the bar, both for yourself and your team. If you reach the pinnacle of what you do, how can you ever come down from that? Do you look at a different pinnacle, or do you raise the bar? In most cases, there is still room to grow no matter how great an achievement you or your team reaches.

Every victory is a notch, not a pinnacle. A mentality that the end goal or mission is bigger than just the project at hand helps to keep people moving and innovating. However, make sure that the end goal is not totally elusive.

Since I started coaching, I've had a philosophy that I have expectations of everyone to get to a point where they know what they're doing and are comfortable with it. When they reach that point, we want to celebrate it and then bump the bar higher and continue to challenge them. Celebration can help drive you to be the best you can be by appreciating how far you've come and then taking another step forward.

You don't want the celebration to become the end goal. In order to maintain intrinsic motivation, the goal you're trying to achieve needs to be worthwhile in and of itself. But if the reward or celebration you tie to that achievement is too big, it can overshadow the goal and change the motivations involved in achieving it.

For example, if you're the leader of a sales team and you offer a new car as a reward to the person who closes the most sales in the year, you may have a highly motivated sales team, but their motivations will be not in doing a great job but in doing whatever they need to increase their numbers. You also create an environment of competition that may cause the team to undermine one another. And since only one person can win the car, you create a sense of resentment in everyone else. These types of rewards, used as motivators, are a terrible way to motivate and celebrate accomplishments.

Aha Moment

Take the preferences of the team into account to ensure that the celebration is meaningful and purposeful.

The goal is to give the team a chance to appreciate one another, to reflect, and to feel a sense of accomplishment. Certain types of celebratory gestures can feel empty if not approached correctly.

You might be familiar with the concept of a "pizza party culture," where leaders recognize their teams through impersonal gestures like a pizza party when the team or organization reaches some goal. Empty gestures of that sort can feel trite or patronizing and build resentment rather than camaraderie—if it's not meaningful to the team, it can do more damage than good.

I've also seen business leaders who fail to recognize that their employees have lives outside of work and choose a celebration in the form of a mandatory after-hours party. Nobody likes mandatory "fun." Sometimes even gestures that may feel generous to the leader can come across as disrespectful and create resentment if they aren't in touch with the real lives of the individuals on the team. While gifting everyone in a company a $100 gift card after a strong year of accomplishments might seem like a nice thing to do, it can backfire and become more damaging than doing nothing at all if it doesn't seem as though the leader's heart is in the right place. If you buy gifts for team members but have your assistant purchase them, wrap them, and deliver them, and then you brag to the media about what you did for your employees, that is likely to breed a lot of resentment because it's frankly disrespectful.

Celebrations must feel meaningful in order to gain their benefits. Just like doing celebrations without thought for the individuals can be damaging, celebrating too often can cause it to lose any meaning.

One of the most effective methods I've seen to handle celebrations is to rotate the responsibility for deciding what and how to celebrate among team members. This brings in different perspectives and helps the team appreciate what each individual is doing and create new opportunities for recognition. It also allows ownership of the celebratory gesture, which can make it feel more meaningful.

TAKEAWAYS

- Celebrating successes builds culture, validates your path, provides a sense of satisfaction, and gives an opportunity to reflect and learn from the journey.

- Celebrations need to be meaningful and purposeful. Celebrating too little or too often can undermine your achievements and be detrimental to your team culture.

- The celebration should never become the end goal. Every victory is a notch, not a pinnacle.

CHAPTER 12

Adapting for Future Risks

"The best way to predict the future is to create it."

–Peter Drucker

The nature of leadership requires constant adapting to change, and it's critical that you know where you want to go and have an adaptable plan to get there. Standard business practices are rapidly changing with innovation, and you have to be ready for what's coming. People are also constantly changing, and they change at different speeds and go in different directions. Part of leadership is thinking about their futures and seeing down the road for each person on your team.

You also need the ability to look out for the future of the team, as well as your department or organization as a whole.

Consider the following questions for yourself and then use them to help your team think about their future together, as well as individually:

- Where are you headed? Is this the path you want to continue?

- Where do you want to be?

- How committed are you to this goal? What is the time frame for realistic achievement?

- What are your distractions? Are they standing in your way or simply excuses?

In the book *Lead From the Future*, authors Mark W. Johnson and Josh Suskewicz describe the visionary leader as one who drives change through those they lead. It's easy to plan ahead with a three-year or five-year plan, but that's not the same thing as leading from the future.

Leading from the future means you're acting as if you're already there. When you understand where you're going in the future, you can identify what needs to happen in order to get there and act in accordance with that.

The future never goes away. It's your job to always keep it in mind and stay on top of current practices, as well as recognizing the difference between a solid current practice and a trend. Trends will mostly lead to a dead end, because they fizzle out over time without a solid direction.

Agility plays an important role in planning for the future. Agility means recognizing that you still have things to learn. I love Brené Brown's book *The Gift of Imperfection*. In it, she discusses how recognizing that you're not perfect and the work you do isn't perfect allows you to continue to learn and seek out new people and resources. If you're not agile enough to search for learning opportunities, your scope will become narrower and narrower as time goes on.

You can make a three-year or five-year plan, but that plan will inevitably change. Many leaders have come to recognize that as they experienced the dramatic changes brought about by the COVID-19 pandemic. It taught many of us valuable lessons about how to prepare for the future.

Because the future is unknown, as a leader you must be willing to take chances, to be bold and daring but not foolish. Ask yourself what you can do differently next, how you can lead differently. The future is unknowable, but we can see better into the near future than the far future, so that informs how you can take chances. That also requires the confidence to be wrong.

You develop the confidence to be wrong by taking chances and learning from them. It's cyclical. Somewhere along the line, you will fail. But what you learn from failing is that it is almost never the end. It's an opportunity to try something different.

RISK

Assessing risks plays a large role in planning for the future, and when you're in a leadership role, there are many factors for you to consider.

Aha Moment

It's impossible to grow or succeed without some level of risk, which is why you must have the confidence to fail.

Especially early in your career, you need the ability to take risks in order to learn from them. But as you grow in leadership, you need to assess risks carefully because what's at stake often affects more than just you.

Typically, when you need to take a risk, it's because there's a circumstance you need to adapt for that requires some level of creativity. And creative solutions always involve some chance of failure, which means that you need your team's buy-in. You don't need their buy-in right away, but you'll need it eventually.

In order to get others on board with your idea or the risk you want to take, I find that one of the best methods is to show them a glimmer of potential through early success. If you believe in it, they will have a better opportunity to believe in it. Leaders have to be strong in their own convictions while listening to the voices of others. This is where it becomes important to listen to your intuition.

RISK ASSESSMENT

Risk can be a guideline in planning for the future, but first you must establish your risk tolerance, or the tolerance of your organization. Your tolerance acts as a guideline to help you assess risk. Coaches and leaders should be able to identify risk and weigh it with all the factors affected, such as people, time, tools or equipment, and legacy.

- **What is the risk, and at whose expense?**

  Who does this risk affect? What is their risk tolerance? When weighing a risk, you must assess not only your own risk tolerance but that of anyone who may be affected. For example, if the risk affects your employees, will it also affect their families? Does it affect the public outside of your organization? In certain industries, this can be the case, and it's vital to take into account the well-being of anyone involved. It is often your team taking the risk, so you must have their interests at heart.

- **What are the possible consequences of this risk, positive and negative?**

  You need to address both the possible benefits and potential drawbacks that could or will occur. This gives you critical information in making a decision, but it is not the only thing you need to consider—great benefit doesn't necessarily always outweigh the drawbacks.

- **Is the risk in the procedures or the outcome?**

  When many people think of risk assessment, they think of outcomes—such as "Will I make money on this investment?" But when you're leading others, often the highest risks are in the procedures to reach your end goal. Will the steps you take be effective? What is the cost of those steps, and what happens if they fail?

- **What is the likelihood of success?**

  Bring data into the equation. Gather as much information as possible. What steps would be necessary to result in success, and how realistic is it that you can achieve those steps?

- **Does the situation warrant such a risk, or is there a safer move we can make?**

  It's necessary to take some risks, but if a decision has particularly high risks, it's often worth it to evaluate if there is another option or if the decision can be adapted to be less risky. What can be decided later, and what must be decided before the process begins? Is there a way to ease in? Many projects can be approached in phases to give you the opportunity to pivot if the decision isn't working out the way you expected.

When you've answered these questions, it's time to start planning how to implement the decision and reach your goal. But the process of assessing risk doesn't stop once you've made the decision. As you begin implementing the steps to get there, you can continue to evaluate how things are going. In the world of sports, wins and losses are finite, but in most organizations, there is some gray area. You can have a win that can be improved upon, or a failure that contains a great deal of success.

When implementing a large project that contains high levels of risk, I like to put in checks to continuously recalculate risk and determine whether it's worth moving forward with the next step. This way, if you hit a wall at one step, you can stop and determine whether something needs to be adjusted to move forward or if the project needs to be abandoned. There has to be a kill switch in place in order to cut your losses if something doesn't go according to plan. Keep the mindset that you can learn and grow from the initial steps you did take even if you don't make it all the way to your goal.

As you begin developing your plan, consider the following:

- What is the desired timeline? Are there any time constraints?

- What will the process or steps look like?

- Who is involved?

- What tools are needed?

- What is the desired outcome? Can there be more than one successful outcome?

- How far are we willing to go? What is your tolerance and what are your boundaries?

- Is this within the organization's expectations, laws, mission, and values?

- What checks and balances are in place?

- Is there a way to ease in, or must you act quickly?

- What are the checkpoints to reassess and adjust if necessary?

- What factors may influence success? What are the chances of success?

Sit with the decision as long as possible and listen to your intuition. Can you own the decision and have your team take action on it? If possible, gather data to support your decision. When you present the decision to your team, you will need to support it—this is different than justifying it. If you made the decision based on your gut or past experience, establish that. If you made it based on data, be clear about that. Don't provide weak support by landing somewhere in the middle.

Aha Moment

In order to make strong decisions, you must have some level of faith in your own judgment and experience, knowing that you've assessed things well and you understand your team, their motivations, and their interests.

DEVELOPING GRIT

The nature of risk is contained in the mysteriousness of the future. Even the best leaders cannot predict everything and will experience failure in spite of assessing their risks well. The way you respond to those failures and coach your team through failures makes all the difference.

Leaders must have grit in order to stay agile, keep pivoting, and make new plans for the future. Over the years, I have developed a clearer definition of grit. Early in my career, it was often used to describe someone who lacked talent but showed a lot of heart or commitment. I didn't know grit until I coached ladies playing softball, sliding and diving in shorts. Ha! That's grit!

The current-day definition of grit has a connotative relationship with coachable features: the drive to finish. Angela Duckworth, the author of *Grit*, defines it as "the determination to do something until you have obtained the skills to do it correctly." That is not the same thing as talent, and it's not the same thing as commitment. It emphasizes the desire to learn and the willingness to struggle in order to grow with an end goal in mind.

Gritty people put in sustained effort over time to achieve a high level of success in their chosen domain. I like this because of the intersection of passion and perseverance. The willingness to recover from failure and try again. The toughness it takes to lead the way, take on a task you've never done before. It means you're willing to fail. Grit pays off in down-to-the-wire situations where cooler heads prevail, because it offers both tenacity and focus.

To me, these are the basic principles of grit:

- A willingness to try without knowing the payoff or outcome

- Doing whatever it takes to overcome an obstacle
- Weighing risks against a successful outcome
- Practicing over and over and making continuous improvements
- Unrelenting self-discipline, intrinsically motivated to accomplish goals
- Surrounding yourself with gritty people

Grit is an essential leadership skill, but it's also something leaders can cultivate in their teams. It starts by setting an example, then helping team members develop confidence and willingness to take risks through positive reinforcement.

Positive reinforcement from a trusted source plays an impactful role in confidence and willingness to take risks. It communicates, "I believe you can do this. If you challenge yourself, you're going to be successful." Positive reinforcement is one of the best tools for leaders because it doesn't focus on punishment, so it allows you to take chances. And by encouraging your team members, you help them learn to try again and again, to live up to your expectations and belief in them, and to develop grit. The more willing they are to fail along the way, the more resilient they'll become.

As a leader, you are training current and future leaders. Each person on your team leads themselves and leads other team members through their actions, attitudes, and values. So as you develop your own leadership style and confidence, you'll help them develop theirs in the process.

TAKEAWAYS

- It's a leader's responsibility to plan for the future of their team and take into account the interests of each person on that team.

- Leading from the future means you're acting as if you're already there.

- In a rapidly changing world, you must stay agile and be willing to take chances, or you will quickly become obsolete.

- When assessing a decision that involves risk, look for opportunities to put checkpoints in place that will allow you to adjust or abandon the plan if the risk factors have changed.

- Leaders with grit are the most likely to succeed in the long term because of their ability to continue to pivot and weather failure.

CONCLUSION

I've always disliked the mantra "fake it till you make it." If you believe you're faking it, you aren't acknowledging the skills you already have to do what you need to do. Many leaders feel insecure, uncertain, or hesitant, and that self-doubt can certainly get in your way. But allowing those feelings to inform your beliefs about yourself will only limit you, or it can cause you to approach situations underprepared because you haven't taken the time to reach for the skills or resources you need.

Over my many years of coaching athletes and business leaders alike, I've seen people allow their insecurities to dictate the way they lead. In every level of leadership, leaders will ascribe their success to someone else, or to some theoretical platform or method rather than their own personal journey. This leads them to become less agile and place blame rather than learn from failure. It makes it difficult to adapt to change because they don't own their processes.

Of course, it's necessary to learn from others, but truly learning means understanding deeply enough to adapt what you've learned into your own leadership methods rather than copying someone else's. So how do you get there? Start by asking questions—my favorite is "why?"

"Why?" is an incredibly powerful question. Here are three of my favorite ways to use it:

1. Ask "why?" when someone is teaching you in order to understand the reasoning behind a lesson. This allows you to gain a fuller understanding and better adapt what you learn to your particular situation.

2. Ask "why" to understand yourself better. Self-awareness is the foundation for experiential leadership. When you're afraid of something, ask yourself why. Interrogate those feelings and where they came from. When you feel motivated toward something, ask yourself why. Understanding your own motivations and values goes a long way to developing your leadership style. When you find a leadership method that does or doesn't work well for you, ask yourself why. The more you get to know yourself, the more confident you'll become in your own leadership.

3. Ask "why" when leading others to gain an understanding of their reasoning and to help them examine their own motivations. Sometimes getting someone to stop and ask this question may result in an epiphany, or it can be the confirmation that's needed to take the next step or overcome the fear of failure.

Most importantly, don't forget to explain your own reasons why when you're asking someone to do something.

I believe every person with a role in any system should understand why they are asked to do what they do.

"Why" can drive you. It can grab the steering wheel and mash the accelerator. It's freedom and an empowerment.

Before you can impart change, make it a priority to create a solid base of understanding your intention—what drives you, what inside you creates a desire to lead, what kind of understanding and change in others you want to see. Leading is a choice built on experience and peppered with risk and doubt. There will always be situations that create fear of failure and self-doubt, but you already have the tools you need to face whatever comes your way.

CONNECT

Kelly Gibbons would like to offer her expertise as an executive leadership coach, facilitator, and workplace trainer to enhance the effectiveness of your leadership team through targeted training or to be the keynote speaker at your next event.

With a focus on addressing your specific needs, Kelly offers speaking, teaching, and coaching sessions. Her areas of specialization include:

- Executive coaching for authentic leadership

- Creating positive team cultures

- Developing new leaders to grow their leadership ability

For inquiries or to initiate a discussion about your event's needs, please reach out to Kelly directly at soulintention@live.com.

If you require books for training sessions, conferences, tradeshows, or events where Kelly is speaking, contact Aloha Publishing at AlohaPublishing@gmail.com for substantial discounts.

Aloha Publishing is committed to prompt responses and efficient delivery of books directly to your company or event location.

ACKNOWLEDGMENTS

I would like to express my sincere gratitude to Maryanna Young for encouraging me and believing in me. Your advice, expertise, and friendship was invaluable throughout the entire book process.

Special thanks to Megan Terry for your writing expertise, encouragement, and assistance. You greatly influenced and enhanced the quality of this book. Your insight is on point.

I would also like to acknowledge my friend and stalwart leadership guide, Ron Price. Thank you for providing me avenues of growth and learning I would not have had otherwise. You were a beacon in times when I needed light.

I am deeply thankful to my parents for their unwavering support and understanding during my coaching journey. Although they are not alive to see the culmination of my life's passion, their emotional support, encouragement, and unconditional love sustained me through all the celebrations and the challenges.

Lastly, a general thank-you to all of my athletes over the years, in the creation, content, and motivation to write this book. Your willingness to listen and learn, your friendship during some of the darkest times in my life, your inspiration through your hard work and grit, and even your dissention is genuinely appreciated. For without you, there would have been no Coach K.

There are many more people to thank, including my kids and grandkids, who have been so inspirational and encouraging and brought out the best of my Coach K side.

ABOUT THE AUTHOR

Kelly Gibbons is an executive leadership coach with over 25 years of coaching experience in both the business and sports realms. Her unique coaching philosophy focuses on the idea that every leader possesses the tools they need to reach their potential. Kelly began her coaching career in women's collegiate volleyball and softball, where she discovered her passion for team leadership and empowerment, a theme she carries into her work in executive leadership in the business and nonprofit spheres.

Kelly graduated from the University of Idaho with a bachelor's degree in public relations and was inducted into the University of Idaho Athletic Hall of Fame in 2009 for volleyball. She earned her master's degree in organizational communications from the University of Kansas. Kelly lives in Idaho and loves the state where she raised her children, who have excelled in sports and academics at the highest levels. Her youngest son, Cole currently attends the University of Idaho.

Kelly's long-term passion is to see leaders, coaches, and professionals at all levels be highly successful in their professional and personal lives.

Made in the USA
Middletown, DE
09 June 2024

55383243R00102